T2-CSE-081

980724

SEP 28 1998 AP 24 '00		
NO 19 '98 MY 1 '99		
NO 23 '98		
MR 22 '99		
AP 26 '99		
AP 28 '99		
AP 30 '99		
MY 03 '99		
OC 14 '99		
OC 25 '99		
NO 8 '99		

CLONING

Other Books in the At Issue Series:

CLONING

David Bender, *Publisher*
Bruno Leone, *Executive Editor*

Brenda Stalcup, *Managing Editor*
Scott Barbour, *Series Editor*

Paul A. Winters, *Book Editor*

An Opposing Viewpoints® Series

Greenhaven Press, Inc.
San Diego, California

Library of Congress Cataloging-in-Publication Data

Cloning / Paul A. Winters, book editor.
      p.   cm. — (At issue)
    Includes bibliographical references and index.
    ISBN 1-56510-753-5 (lib.: alk. paper). — ISBN 1-56510-752-7
(pbk. : alk. paper)
    1. Cloning—Moral and ethical aspects. I. Winters, Paul A.,
1965– . II. Series: At issue (San Diego, Calif.)
QH442.2.C56   1998
174'.957—dc21   97-28560
                                                                  CIP

© 1998 by Greenhaven Press, Inc., PO Box 289009,
              San Diego, CA 92198-9009

              Printed in the U.S.A.

Every effort has been made to trace owners of copyrighted material.

Table of Contents

Introduction

In February 1997, Ian Wilmut and his colleagues at the Roslin Institute in Scotland announced the stunning news that they had cloned a lamb from the cells of a mature sheep. Although many animal cloning experiments had been performed in the past, they had succeeded only in cloning the cells of embryos. This latest experiment was remarkable because it was the first successful attempt to clone a mature mammal, producing an exact physical replica of the adult animal.

Wilmut and his lamb, whom the researchers named Dolly, became instant celebrities and found themselves at the center of intense debate. However, the uproar that resulted from the scientists' announcement was focused not on the creation of Dolly, but on the possible application of cloning technology to other mammals—specifically humans. Indeed, the arrival of Dolly brought the realization, as the British scientific journal *Nature* stated, that "cloning humans from adults' tissues is likely to be achievable any time from one to ten years from now." The news of Dolly's birth therefore led to a great deal of discussion about the scientific, moral, and ethical issues surrounding the prospect of human cloning.

The science of cloning

In normal mammalian reproduction, sperm and egg fuse naturally, each contributing half of the material that makes up a genetically unique individual. In the process that was used to create Dolly, known as gene transfer, scientists mechanically fused a cell from one animal onto an enucleated egg cell—that is, an egg cell whose nucleus (which contains the cell's DNA) has been removed. Because the egg cell lacks DNA, the embryo that is created contains DNA from only one source. Thus, the embryo will develop into an exact physical replica of the animal from which the cell containing the DNA was taken.

Prior to the creation of Dolly, scientists had thought that gene transfer could only be performed using embryonic cells, in which all the genes are active. They believed that the process could not be conducted using adult cells because in these cells some genes are active and others are inactive. However, Wilmut and his colleagues discovered a way to make adult cells behave like embryonic cells. They then fused 277 nuclei from adult Finn Dorset ewes onto enucleated egg cells taken from Scottish Blackface Ewes. Thirty of the eggs developed into embryos, and twenty-nine of these embryos were implanted into Blackface ewes. One of these pregnancies was carried to term and resulted in the birth of a Finn Dorset lamb, Dolly, who was the exact replica of the adult from which the cell had been taken.

Dolly would seem to be proof that it is possible to perform gene transfer using adult cells, thereby cloning an adult mammal. But as the scientists readily admit, the fact that only one live sheep was born out of twenty-nine tries is a shaky basis for such a conclusion. Confirmation of the success of this breakthrough in cloning technology therefore relies on the reproduction of this experiment by independent researchers. As *Time* magazine correspondent Sharon Begley reports, though, that confirmation may come quickly, as scientists in America and Europe attempt similar cloning experiments with cattle, sheep, and rabbits.

The ethical implications

Wilmut and his colleagues had only envisioned that their technique would be used on animals in the areas of animal husbandry and biomedical science. However, the British government immediately cut its financial support of research at the Roslin Institute until the cloning technology's possible applications to humans could be considered. In the United States, President Bill Clinton announced an immediate moratorium on federal funding of cloning research, arguing that "science often moves faster than our ability to understand its implications." He then requested the National Bioethics Advisory Commission (NBAC) to study the ethical and legal aspects of the issue and to present him with a report containing recommendations for future action by the government. The NBAC held public hearings on the issue in March and April of 1997 and invited comments from scientists, ethicists, religious leaders, and others concerned with the controversy.

Opponents of human cloning believe that it could have numerous negative consequences for society. For example, individuals might have themselves cloned in order to have "spare parts" for organ transplants. Parents might use cloning as a means of replacing a dead or dying child. Some people might be motivated to create clones of famous or extremely talented people. Moreover, many argue, cloning could start society on a "slippery slope" toward attempts to perfect the human race by reproducing genetically "superior" individuals—such as people who are highly intelligent and attractive—and stigmatizing people with genetically "inferior" traits. These and additional social concerns have been expressed by numerous commentators and ethicists in the wake of Dolly's birth.

Other arguments against cloning focus on the implications for the children who would be produced in cloning experiments. For example, some ethicists emphasize the physical danger that the technology poses to these children. Leon R. Kass, a professor at the University of Chicago, contends that cloning experiments on humans are likely to produce "mishaps and deformities" similar to those that result from research on animals. Kass is among those who insist that due to the possibility of creating deformed children, human cloning experiments are unacceptable.

In addition to the risk of physical dangers, some ethicists assert that cloning is unacceptable because it would violate the human dignity of cloned children. Because cloned children would essentially be manufactured rather than conceived, they could potentially be viewed by society as commodities and treated as less than fully human, these critics maintain. According to Gilbert Meilaender of Valparaiso University, "To beget a child is to give birth to one who is like us, equal in dignity, for whom we care, but whose being we do not simply control. To 'make' a child is

to create a product whose destiny we may well think we can shape."
Moreover, critics argue, because a cloned child would inherit the exact
DNA of an existing person rather than a blending of DNA from two
sources, the child would be robbed of the genetic uniqueness that is
essential for the formation of a distinct identity.

However, ethicists and scientists who support further research maintain that the dangers posed by human cloning have been exaggerated.
They argue that many of the predictions made by opponents are unrealistic "science-fiction" scenarios. For example, in response to the fear that
people might create clones for spare parts, supporters of human cloning
research counter that cloned humans would be no different from humans
produced through other means of reproduction and therefore would not
be treated any differently. According to Robert Wachbroit, "Regardless of
the reason that someone has a clone produced, the result would nevertheless be a human being with all the rights and protections that accompany that status."

Many contend that cloning could become a viable alternative means
of reproduction. For example, Ruth Macklin, a professor of bioethics at
Albert Einstein College of Medicine, argues that cloning could provide an
option for infertile couples or for couples in which one partner has a
genetic defect that could be passed on to the child. Alun M. Anderson,
editor of *New Scientist* magazine, concedes that the prospect of a child's
having the identical genetic makeup of one of his or her parents might
seem strange, but he suggests that it "might not be that difficult an idea
to get used to. After all, no one finds twins or even triplets too strange to
deal with." According to many scientists, such potential benefits of
human cloning far outweigh the possible negative consequences and warrant further exploration through research.

After hearing arguments on both sides of the cloning issue, the NBAC
delivered its report and recommendations to the president in June 1997.
The commission called for a three- to five-year continuation of the moratorium on research designed to create a cloned child. The cloning process
is unsafe to be used on humans at present, the commissioners maintained,
and the continued moratorium would give scientists a chance to perfect
the technique. This time could also be used to educate the public about
the technology involved in cloning and to encourage widespread debate
about cloning's moral and ethical implications, the commission wrote.
Commission members argued that cloning research with human cell tissue should be allowed to proceed, as should animal research that met with
guidelines on the ethical treatment of animals. The president accepted the
proposal to leave the moratorium on human research in place.

Debate over the implications of this scientific innovation—especially
the seemingly impending possibility of human cloning—continues in
many quarters. As noted by a legal ethicist who presented testimony at
the NBAC hearings, this is one of the rare occasions when the ethics of a
scientific advancement can be discussed and debated before it becomes a
reality. *At Issue: Cloning* presents a variety of opinions on the moral, ethical, and legal issues surrounding cloning.

1

Human Cloning
Would Be Unethical

John O'Connor

John O'Connor, a Roman Catholic cardinal, is the archbishop of New York.

The cloning of a human being would be unethical because it would not serve any necessary or beneficial medical purpose. The research needed to develop human cloning would produce many imperfect results, and it would be sinful to simply dispose of these "mistakes." In addition, if humans were successfully cloned, such persons would have no parents and would therefore be less than fully human in status. Further, scientists simply do not have the wisdom to direct the course of evolution.

We support all true progress in conventional medicine. It is common in biomedical literature to distinguish negative from positive genetic engineering. *Negative* genetic engineering cures a disease, removes a defect or alleviates a pathology. This is the tradition of Western medicine, and all progress in that tradition is welcome. However, *positive* genetic engineering is the construction and/or manufacture of a higher or better type of human (e.g., replication—i.e., cloning—of a "superior" type or trait). This is not truly therapeutic; it is not genuine medicine; it is not human progress and is not welcome.

Science should serve humanity

The distinction is not anti-science; it is rather a plea for socially responsible and socially accountable science. Science that serves and enhances the human person is welcome: What serves the human person upholds a criterion of respect, generosity and service while resisting the slide to a new criterion of efficiency, functionality and usefulness.

I offer no comment on subhuman cloning. Many see this only as high-tech animal husbandry, but even there the potential danger of a

From John O'Connor, "Human Cloning: Efficiency vs. Ethics," *Origins*, April 10, 1997. Reprinted courtesy of the Catholic News Service.

genetic cul de sac needs study. The strength of evolution is its diversity, not its sameness.

The present and pressing question before us is human cloning—the seriousness of which is obvious to all. This is not research to improve "salad oil" or research to improve "motor oil," this is something new and gravely important because the focus is human—the object, the subject, the means and the stakes are human!

A technological imperative, with blinders on and earplugs in place, might suggest, "Whatever can be done, should be done!" That slogan demands close scrutiny.

Permit me to submit a few basic objections to human cloning. First, it is a drastic invasion of human parenthood. A clone technically has no human parents, not by accident, but by design. This does disrespect both to the dignity of human procreation and the dignity of the conjugal union (marriage). Contrary to the right of every human person to be conceived and born within marriage and from marriage (*Donum Vitae*, 1, 6), the clone is reduced to the level of a product made rather than a person begotten.

The clone is reduced to the level of a product made rather than a person begotten.

Throughout our nation's history, the Judeo-Christian tradition has respected the divine design of life-giving love ("and the two become one flesh" Gn. 2:24; Mk. 10:8; Eph. 5:31). In the process of cloning, this personal, unitive, two-in-one-flesh dimension of life-giving marital love is rejected and replaced by technological replication. Begetting is the continuation of creation (*Evangelium Vitae*, 43); manufacturing is proper to and productive of things, not persons.

To reduce human procreation to no more, no better or no different than plant or animal replication—without human parenthood—is to remove the *humanum* from human parents and the human child. (The potential psychological consequences, proximate and remote, for both clone and cloner are simply unknown. But with humans it is not enough not to know we do harm; with humans we must know that we cause no harm. The first canon of medical ethics remains: *primum non nocere!* First, do no harm!).

A second basic objection to human cloning is on the level of human wisdom. Take a sober look at our external environment. Consider the man-made damage done to our natural external environment, some foreseen, much unforeseen. Is any serious person that sanguine about the state of our external environment that he or she is positively anxious now to "engineer" our internal human evolution? Do we have the wisdom? The Scottish cloned sheep, Dolly, came into being on the 300th attempt. The first 277 attempts did not even fuse. From 278 to 299 they did fuse but misguided, misshaped, grew a bit and essentially fell apart. Switch focus to human beings. No. 1 try is blue-eyed. Wrong color. Only brown is acceptable. Oops, I wanted a boy. Get rid of this girl. Etc., etc., etc. How many human beings are destroyed before the ideal is achieved? Ideal according to whose standards? Do we throw away human beings like paper napkins?

Does anyone think some expert is going to hit a perfect human clone on the first and only try? What are we to do with or say of the "mishaps," the "mistakes," the less-than-perfect tries and results? Do we just discard them as "near misses," as with research for improved salad or motor oil? What is their human status? What is their legal status? Have they any protections or protectors, or are they mere biological stuff?

In the process of "making" a clone, just who is in charge of quality control? What qualifications are relevant to quality controllers, and who in our society possesses the qualifications to determine who can or cannot enter our human community? (For early eugenic elimination, cf. *Evangelium Vitae,* 14, 63.)

At least in human procreation there is a natural community (mother and father) to receive new life. In human cloning, it is not truly the "parent(s)" who decide but the technicians who determine which "quality types" qualify for membership in the human community.

Is this limited to the married? Is it limited to one sex or the other? Is there a controllable agenda to preclude one sex or the other?

The third basic objection to human cloning includes social and ethical questions. Cloning is not now and never will be a poor people's campaign. Could it be or become an entitlement requiring public subsidy? This is a most undesirable shift because it replaces ethical categories with manufacturing imperatives. The act of human cloning itself cures no pathology. Thus, we are not doctoring the patient but doctoring the race.

The value of a child's life

There remains a profound ethical difference between "having a child" and "making a child." A child begotten can always be seen as a gift, whereas a child made or manufactured can always be seen as a thing—a product for use, not to be respected for what he/she is, but priced for what it can do, have or be used for. That is no way to treat or value a human being.

In this shift, the scientific canons of efficiency replace the ethics of life. That is a giant societal step in the wrong direction. It is ironic that now, near the close of the 20th century, a century that spent great time and effort to have sex without babies, now some want to have babies without sex.

What are we to do with or say of the "mishaps," the "mistakes," the less-than-perfect tries and results?

To summarize, scientific developments at the service of the human person are welcome. We rejoice in God-given genius and applications that have materially improved the lives of us all. However, not every scientific application of our century has been put to good use; some have been put to tragic misuse, even catastrophic misuse on a scale no prior century could dream of or realize.

Research proposals are not value-neutral, and those that are hostile to

12 *At Issue*

human parenthood, unknown in deleterious human consequences and cure no disease, these are not medicine and are not welcome. It is simply not acceptable to say, "I only work in a lab; I only do research; I'm not into philosophy or ethics or politics." This is a matter of great social and human responsibility.

Let us conclude and concur with the late Paul Ramsey, who stated clearly: "The good things that men do can be made complete only by the things they refuse to do." (*Fabricated Man: The Ethics of Genetic Control*, p. 123).

2

Human Cloning Would Violate Christian Ethics

John F. Kilner

John F. Kilner is director of the Center for Bioethics and Human Dignity in Bannockburn, Illinois.

Human cloning research would be unethical because it would inevitably cause the deaths of human embryos. Further, cloning a human for a particular purpose would violate that person's God-given human dignity by subordinating his or her existence to the interests of others. Cloning research should not be permitted for any purpose.

C igar, the champion racehorse, is a dud as a stud. Attempts to impregnate numerous mares have failed. But his handlers are not discouraged. They think they might try to have Cigar cloned.

If a sheep and a monkey can be cloned—and possibly a racehorse—can human clones be far behind? The process is novel, though the concept is not.

We have long known that virtually every cell of the body contains a person's complete genetic code. The exception is sperm or egg cells, each of which contains half the genetic material until the sperm fertilizes the egg and a new human being with a complete genetic code begins growing.

We have now learned that the partial genetic material in an unfertilized egg cell may be replaced by the complete genetic material from a cell taken from an adult. With a full genetic code, the egg cell behaves as if it has been fertilized. At least, that is how Dolly, the sheep cloned in Scotland, came to be. Hence, producing genetic copies of human beings now seems more likely.

The costs of clones

We have been anticipating this possibility in humans for decades and have been playing with it in our imaginations. The movie *The Boys from Brazil* was about an attempt to clone Adolf Hitler. And in Aldous Huxley's

From John F. Kilner, "Stop Cloning Around," *Christianity Today*, April 28, 1997. Reprinted by permission of the author.

novel *Brave New World,* clones were produced to fulfill undesirable social roles. More recently the movie *Multiplicity* portrayed a harried man who jumped at the chance to have himself copied—the better to tend to his office work, his home chores, and his family relationships. It all seems so attractive, at first glance, in our hectic, achievement-crazed society.

As movies and novels suggest, and godly wisdom confirms, human cloning is something neither to fool around with nor to attempt.

But how do we achieve this technologically blissful state? *Multiplicity* is silent on this matter, implying that technique is best left to scientists, as if the rest of us are interested only in the outcome. But the experiments of Nazi Germany and the resulting Nuremberg Trials and Code taught us long ago that there is some knowledge that we must not pursue if it requires the use of immoral means.

The research necessary to develop human cloning will cause the deaths of human beings. Such deaths make the cost unacceptably high. In the process used to clone sheep, there were 277 failed attempts—including the deaths of several defective clones. In the monkey-cloning process, a living embryo was intentionally destroyed by taking the genetic material from the embryo's eight cells and inserting it into eight egg cells whose partial genetic material had been removed. Human embryos and human infants would likewise be lost as the technique is adapted to our own race.

Goal rush

Yet, as we press toward this new mark, we must ask: Is the production of human clones even a worthwhile goal? As movies and novels suggest, and godly wisdom confirms, human cloning is something neither to fool around with nor to attempt.

Cloning typically involves genetically copying some living thing for a particular purpose—a wheat plant that yields much grain, a cow that provides excellent milk. Such utilitarian approaches may be fine for cows and corn, but human beings, made in the image of God, have a God-given dignity that prevents us from regarding other people merely as means to fulfill our desires. We must not, for instance, produce clones with low intelligence (or low ambition) to provide menial labor, or produce clones to provide transplantable organs (their identical genetic code would minimize organ rejection). We should not even clone a child who dies tragically in order to remove the parents' grief, as if the clone could actually *be* the child who died.

All people are special creations of God who should be loved and respected as such. We must not demean them by fundamentally subordinating their interests to those of others.

There is a host of problems with human cloning that we have yet to address. Who are the parents of a clone produced in a laboratory? The donor of the genetic material? The donor of the egg into which the material is transferred? The scientist who manipulates cells from anonymous donors? Who will provide the necessary love and care for this embryo, fetus, and then child—especially when mistakes are made and it would be easier simply to discard *it*?

The problems become legion when having children is removed from the context of marriage and even from responsible parenthood. For instance, Hope College's Allen Verhey asks "whether parenting is properly considered making children to match a specific design, as is clearly the case with cloning, or whether parenting is properly regarded as a disposition to be hospitable to children as given." Clearly, from a biblical perspective, it is the latter.

When human cloning becomes technically possible, who will control who clones whom and for what ends?

Further, the Bible portrays children as the fruit of a one-flesh love relationship, and for good reason. It is a context in which children flourish—in which their full humanity, material and nonmaterial, is respected and nourished. Those who provide them with physical (genetic) life also care for their ongoing physical as well as nonphysical needs.

As Valparaiso University's Gilbert Meilaender told *Christianity Today*, this further separation of procreating from marriage is bad for children. "The child inevitably becomes a product," says ethicist Meilaender, someone who is made, not begotten.

"To beget a child is to give birth to one who is like us, equal in dignity, for whom we care, but whose being we do not simply control. To 'make' a child is to create a product whose destiny we may well think we can shape. Hence, the 'begotten, not made' language of the creed is relevant also to our understanding of the child and of the relation between the generations.

"If our purpose is to clone people as possible sources of perfectly matching organs," says Meilaender, "that clearly shows how we could come to regard the clone as a being we control—as simply an 'ensemble of parts or organs.'"

Xeroxing Michael

It is all too easy to lose sight of the fact that people are more than just physical beings, Meilaender's ensembles of organs. What most excites many people about cloning is the possibility of duplicate Michael Jordans, Mother Teresas, or Colin Powells. However, were clones of any of these heroes to begin growing today, those clones would not turn out to be our heroes, for our heroes are not who they are simply because of their DNA. They, like us, were shaped by genetics and environment alike, with the spiritual capacity to evaluate, disregard, and at times to overcome either or both. Each clone would be subject to a unique set of environmental influences, and our loving God would surely accord each a unique personal relationship with him.

The problem with cloning is not the mere fact that technology is involved. Technology can help us do better what God has for us to do. The problem arises when we use technology for purposes that conflict with God's. And, as C.S. Lewis argued, technology never merely represents human mastery over nature; it also involves the power of some people over other people. This is as true in the genetic revolution as it was in the Industrial Revolution. When human cloning becomes technically possible, who will control who clones whom and for what ends? Like nuclear weaponry, the power to clone in the "wrong hands" could have devastating consequences.

There is wisdom in President Clinton's immediate move to forestall human cloning research until public debate and expert testimony have been digested and policies formulated. But there is even greater wisdom in never setting foot on the path that leads from brave new sheep to made-to-order organ donors, industrial drones, and vanity children.

3

Cloning Would Violate Human Dignity

Martin E. Marty

Martin E. Marty, senior editor of the Christian Century *magazine, is a professor of the history of religion at the University of Chicago and director of the Public Religion Project, a nonprofit group that analyzes the role of religion in American life.*

The common reactions to the prospect of human cloning are revulsion and fear, but these feelings are based on deeper concerns. Though reproductive technologies have been applauded in the past because they produce children, cloning is different. Cloning assaults the distinctive genetic individuality of humans in a way that other reproductive technologies do not.

A n instinct by humans to protect their distinctiveness is evident in the first responses to the announcement that a scientist in Scotland has cloned an adult sheep. The biologist Ian Wilmut and the sheep Dolly have become instantly familiar figures. At once, respondents to the news speculated about human cloning. Not "whether" the technique will be applied to humans but "when" and "what then" have framed most questions.

Reactions to the prospect of human cloning

Guarding what is left of human distinctiveness has to be at issue. Otherwise, why not greet this discovery the way citizens greet so many scientific breakthroughs? The public cheered when astronauts walked on the moon. It honors those who move us closer to cancer cures. True, some scientific production has only baleful effects. No one cheers chemical and bacterial warfare. Other scientific ventures evoke ambiguity. The Human Genome Project will advance health. But, after it, will people refuse to hire people if a reading of their genetic catalogs suggests bad times ahead?

Human-cloning notions awaken responses somewhere between outright dismissal of malignity and expressions of great fear about ambiguity. Dr. Harold E. Varmus, director of the National Institutes of Health,

From Martin E. Marty, "What About the Exalted Individual?" *Los Angeles Times*, March 2, 1997. Reprinted by permission of the author.

appeared before a congressional committee to plead that lawmakers not slam the door on all cloning research. But he hurried to add that "cloning of an existing human being is repugnant to the American people." Just as typical was the comment of Alexander Capron of the University of Southern California and the National Bioethics Advisory Commission. He looked at the con's and pro's of human cloning and pronounced: "I don't see the pros, frankly."

Philosophers and theologians weighed in with virtually unanimous "con" pronouncements. They joined the interviewed public who, on camera, turned up their noses and turned down their thumbs when asked whether they would favor making genetic twins of children. Listen carefully to them, and you will hear that the reason most have fewer reservations about sheep and other animal cloning than they do about experiments with people is their fear that what is distinctively human will be assaulted again.

The folk language draws on cliches such as "you shouldn't fool with Mother Nature" or "you shouldn't play God." But even the verbs "fool" and "play" are a bit too light this time around. The crossing of this new scientific horizon produced intuitions that science now possesses the key to a door of discovery that most would rather have seen forever locked.

Ambiguity and uncertainty

Human distinctiveness, of course, has never been absolute. First, the connection between the cloning of the mammal Dolly and the prospect of similarly reproducing humans is one more illustration of the kinship people have with animals and the natural world as a whole.

Second, much of what goes on in the laboratory, especially in clinics that serve the infertile, already appears at the edges of what many conceive to be limits set down by Nature and God alike. When doctors and members of the public use in-vitro fertilization procedures, they do so to serve one of the strongest and most admirable human drives: for adults to become parents. We cheer the resultant births of distinctive babies, but have still not faced all that the techniques themselves may come to mean. Best guesses are that the first word about "pro's" in human cloning will come from aspiring parents and the enterprising clinics that would serve them. On that front, the window of ambiguity is likely to open a bit.

Science now possesses the key to a door of discovery that most would rather have seen forever locked.

Third, as in the laboratory, so in the study, there are uncertainties about what we mean when we speak of distinctive humanness. Scientists join philosophers and theologians in controversy over how to connect the physical brain with the mind and thus with consciousness and—gasp!—soul. Debates over this nexus are among the liveliest—and they are as promising and threatening as they are likely to remain irresolvable.

The implied language of reducing, of reductionism, is clear here. In that language, we are "nothing but . . ." this or that. Nothing but the selfish gene seeking social evolutionary expression; nothing but awesomely complex living computers with legs; nothing but material beings who live to eat and propagate. Most of these contentions include elements of plausibility. Nonexperts are no more capable of simply refuting them than are experts prone to agree with each other in their "nothing-but" conflicts.

Defining human distinctiveness

When striving to guard human distinctiveness, words like "intuition" and "instinct" are most appropriate. To them, one could add words like "wager" and "faith." The impulse to use one language for science and another for faith, one for the need to discover and another for the stewardship of what is already precious, one for precision about what is knowable and another for what has to be envisioned—all these do not necessarily produce fractured psyches. They represent different modes by which humans pursue what is valuable to them. Being concerned about the future of the human race does not have to be written off to pride or insecurity, to anti-animal self-concern, to ignorance of science. Attribute it to what E.M. Forster called the effort to provide "breathing holes for the human spirit."

If the debates over human cloning force the often neglectful to reexamine and reform themselves, the years before human cloning will be better spent.

When most people in our culture speak of human distinctiveness, they affirm that people are subjects of divine creation, a concept they freely interpret in more ways than there are sects and schools. Political scientist Glenn Tinder, who has tried to focus religious concern in politics on a few specific concepts, promotes "the prophetic community," in which believers speak out and act together for human good against all dehumanizing odds. He adds that proclaiming that we are made "in the image of God" means concern for what he calls the "exalted individual." This creature is not Nietzsche's "man-God." In fact, when Tinder speaks to Christians, he reminds them that their dignity is reinforced by Jesus, seen as the human in whom God distinctively "dwells." That ought to make a difference in their own humaneness.

You don't have to be a believer in any part of the Bible to care for "the exalted individual," that person who can be forgotten if reduced to employable genes in the cloning lab. Here those who care about Mother Nature and about God sharpen ethical concerns.

When twins share a womb and then a life, they are expressions of freedom, contingency, luck or providence. We take our chances. If, in the future, a twin can be "artificially" produced as a member of the next generation, this would be an expression of aspiring mastery and control, a taking command that might undercut the dignity and integrity of the human—at least as we have known humans.

To write about ill-defined responses to a hard-to-envision set of challenges is not to suggest that those who now respond to the deepest themes of philosophy or the strongest call of God have done all they could in the past to protect the distinctively human. Too many have engaged in slavery and repression. They have promoted inquisition and caused indignity, have exploited and manipulated others. They stand accused of having neglected the natural and social environments in which noncloned offspring had to make their way.

If the debates over human cloning force the often neglectful to reexamine and reform themselves, the years before human cloning will be better spent. Such acts are more creative than are mere expressions of repugnance and quaking. Human cloning is about generations being genetically like each other. Debate about it has to do also with generations being truly different from each other, and their members being exalted individuals—free and distinctive.

4

Human Cloning Would Violate the Dignity of Children

Gilbert Meilaender

Gilbert Meilaender holds the Board of Directors Chair in Theological Ethics at Valparaiso University in Indiana.

Protestant Christian belief maintains that children should be the product of the sexual union of a man and a woman united in marriage, not only because this arrangement is in the best interest of the child but because it is in the interests of the man and woman as well. When children are begotten through the sexual union of two parents, they are equal in humanity to the parents. But if they were to be made by the parents through cloning, they would be robbed of this dignity. Cloning would give to parents the power to determine the genetic makeup of their children—a power that would be unethical to exercise.

Editor's note: The following remarks were presented to the National Bioethics Advisory Commission on March 13, 1997.

I have been invited, as I understand it, to speak today specifically as a Protestant theologian. I have tried to take that charge seriously, and I have chosen my concerns accordingly. I do not suppose, therefore, that the issues I address are the only issues to which you ought to give your attention. Thus, for example, I will not address the question of whether we could rightly conduct the first experiments in human cloning, given the likelihood that such experiments would not at first fully succeed. That is an important moral question, but I will not take it up. Nor do I suppose that I can represent Protestants generally. There is no such beast. Indeed, Protestants are specialists in the art of fragmentation. In my own tradition, which is Lutheran, we commonly understand ourselves as quite content to be Catholic except when, on certain questions, we are compelled to disagree. Other Protestants might think of themselves differently.

From Gilbert Meilaender, "Begetting and Cloning," *First Things*, June/July 1997. Reprinted by permission of *First Things*.

More important, however, is this point: Attempting to take my charge seriously, I will speak theologically—not just in the standard language of bioethics or public policy. I do not think of this, however, simply as an opportunity for the "Protestant interest group" to weigh in at your deliberations. On the contrary, this theological language has sought to uncover what is universal and human. It begins epistemologically from a particular place, but it opens up ontologically a vision of the human. The unease about human cloning that I will express is widely shared. I aim to get at some of the theological underpinnings of that unease in language that may seem unfamiliar or even unwelcome, but it is language that is grounded in important Christian affirmations that seek to understand the child as our equal—one who is a gift and not a product. In any case, I will do you the honor of assuming that you are interested in hearing what those who speak such a language have to say, and I will also suppose that a faith which seeks understanding may sometimes find it.

Lacking an accepted teaching office within the church, Protestants had to find some way to provide authoritative moral guidance. They turned from the authority of the church as interpreter of Scripture to the biblical texts themselves. That characteristic Protestant move is not likely, of course, to provide any very immediate guidance on a subject such as human cloning. But it does teach something about the connection of marriage and parenthood. The creation story in the first chapter of Genesis depicts the creation of humankind as male and female, sexually differentiated and enjoined by God's grace to sustain human life through procreation.

The biblical significance of marriage and children

Hence, there is given in creation a connection between the differentiation of the sexes and the begetting of a child. We begin with that connection, making our way indirectly toward the subject of cloning. It is from the vantage point of this connection that our theological tradition has addressed two questions that are both profound and mysterious in their simplicity: What is the meaning of a child? And what is good for a child? These questions are, as you know, at the heart of many problems in our society today, and it is against the background of such questions that I want to reflect upon the significance of human cloning. What Protestants found in the Bible was a normative view: namely, that the sexual differentiation is ordered toward the creation of offspring, and children should be conceived within the marital union. By God's grace the child is a gift who springs from the giving and receiving of love. Marriage and parenthood are connected—held together in a basic form of humanity.

To this depiction of the connection between sexual differentiation and child-bearing as normative, it is, as Anglican theologian Oliver O'Donovan has argued, possible to respond in different ways. We may welcome the connection and find in it humane wisdom to guide our conduct. We may resent it as a limit to our freedom and seek to transcend it. We did not need modern scientific breakthroughs to know that it is possible—and sometimes seemingly desirable—to sever the connection between marriage and begetting children. The possibility of human cloning is striking only because it breaks the connection so emphatically. It aims directly at the heart of the mystery that is a child. Part of the mystery here is that we will always be hard-pressed to explain why the connection of sexual differentiation and procreation should not be broken. Precisely to the degree that it is a basic form of humanity, it will be hard to give more fundamental reasons why the connection should be welcomed and honored when, in our freedom, we need not do so. But moral argument must begin somewhere. To see through everything is, as C.S. Lewis once put it, the same as not to see at all.

If we cannot argue to this starting point, however, we can argue from it. If we cannot entirely explain the mystery, we can explicate it. And the explication comes from two angles. Maintaining the connection between procreation and the sexual relationship of a man and woman is good both for that relationship and for children.

It is good, first, for the relation of the man and woman. No doubt the motives of those who beget children coitally are often mixed, and they may be uncertain about the full significance of what they do. But if they are willing to shape their intentions in accord with the norm I have outlined, they may be freed from self-absorption. The act of love is not simply a personal project undertaken to satisfy one's own needs, and procreation, as the fruit of coitus, reminds us of that. Even when the relation of a man and woman does not or cannot give rise to offspring, they can understand their embrace as more than their personal project in the world, as their participation in a form of life that carries its own inner meaning and has its telos established in the creation. The meaning of what we do then is not determined simply by our desire or will. As Oliver O'Donovan has noted, some understanding like this is needed if the sexual relation of a man and woman is to be more than "simply a profound form of play."

And when the sexual act becomes only a personal project, so does the child. No longer then is the bearing and rearing of children thought of as a task we should take up or as a return we make for the gift of life; instead, it is a project we undertake if it promises to meet our needs and desires. Those people—both learned commentators and ordinary folk—who in recent days have described cloning as narcissistic or as replication of one's self see something important. Even if we grant that a clone, reared in different circumstances than its immediate ancestor, might turn out to be quite a different person in some respects, the point of that person's existence would be grounded in our will and desire.

Maintaining the connection between procreation and the sexual relationship of a man and woman is good both for that relationship and for children.

Hence, retaining the tie that unites procreation with the sexual relation of a man and woman is also good for children. Even when a man and woman deeply desire a child, the act of love itself cannot take the child as its primary object. They must give themselves to each other, setting aside their projects, and the child becomes the natural fruition of their shared love—something quite different from a chosen project. The child is therefore always a gift—one like them who springs from their embrace, not a being whom they have made and whose destiny they should determine. This is light-years away from the notion that we all have a right to have children—in whatever way we see fit, whenever it serves our purposes. Our children begin with a kind of genetic independence of us, their parents. They replicate neither their father nor their mother. That is a reminder of the independence that we must eventually grant to them and for which it is our duty to prepare them. To lose, even in principle, this sense of the child as a gift entrusted to us will not be good for children.

The distinction between making and begetting

I will press this point still further by making one more theological move. When Christians tried to tell the story of Jesus as they found it in their Scriptures, they were driven to some rather complex formulations. They wanted to say that Jesus was truly one with that God whom he called Father, lest it should seem that what he had accomplished did not really overcome the gulf that separates us from God. Thus, while distinguishing the persons of Father and Son, they wanted to say that Jesus is truly God—of one being with the Father. And the language in which they did this (in the fourth-century Nicene Creed, one of the two most important creeds that antedate the division of the church in the West at the Reformation) is language which describes the Son of the Father as "begotten, not made." Oliver O'Donovan has noted that this distinction between making and begetting, crucial for Christians' understanding of God, carries considerable moral significance.

What the language of the Nicene Creed wanted to say was that the Son is God just as the Father is God. It was intended to assert an equality of being. And for that what was needed was a language other than the language of making. What we beget is like ourselves. What we make is not; it is the product of our free decision, and its destiny is ours to determine. Of course, on this Christian understanding human beings are not begotten in the absolute sense that the Son is said to be begotten of the Father. They are made—but made by God through human begetting. Hence, although we are not God's equal, we are of equal dignity with each other. And we are not at each other's disposal. If it is, in fact, human begetting that expresses our equal dignity, we should not lightly set it aside in a manner as decisive as cloning.

If it is, in fact, human begetting that expresses our equal dignity, we should not lightly set it aside in a manner as decisive as cloning.

I am well aware, of course, that other advances in what we are pleased to call reproductive technology have already strained the connection between the sexual relationship of a man and woman and the birth of a child. Clearly, procreation has to some extent become reproduction, making rather than doing. I am far from thinking that all this has been done well or wisely, and sometimes we may only come to understand the nature of the road we are on when we have already traveled fairly far along it. But whatever we say of that, surely human cloning would be a new and decisive turn on this road—far more emphatically a kind of production, far less a surrender to the mystery of the genetic lottery which is the mystery of the child who replicates neither father nor mother but incarnates their union, far more an understanding of the child as a product of human will.

I am also aware that we can all imagine circumstances in which we ourselves might—were the technology available—be tempted to turn to cloning. Parents who lose a young child in an accident and want to "replace" her. A seriously ill person in need of embryonic stem cells to repair damaged tissue. A person in need of organs for transplant. A person who is infertile and wants, in some sense, to reproduce. Once the child becomes a project or product, such temptations become almost irresistible. There is no end of good causes in the world, and they would sorely tempt us even if we did not live in a society for which the pursuit of health has become a god, justifying almost anything.

As theologian and bioethicist William F. May has often noted, we are preoccupied with death and the destructive powers of our world. But without in any way glorifying suffering or pretending that it is not evil, Christians worship a God who wills to be with us in our dependence, teaching us "attentiveness before a good and nurturant God." We learn therefore that what matters is how we live, not only how long—that we are responsible to do as much good as we can, but this means, as much as we can within the limits morality sets for us.

I am also aware, finally, that we might for now approve human cloning but only in restricted circumstances—as, for example, the cloning of preimplantation embryos (up to fourteen days) for experimental use. That would, of course, mean the creation solely for purposes of research of human embryos—human subjects who are not really best described as preimplantation embryos. They are unimplanted embryos—a locution that makes clear the extent to which their being and destiny are the product of human will alone. If we are genuinely baffled about how best to describe the moral status of that human subject who is the unimplanted embryo, we should not go forward in a way that peculiarly combines metaphysical bewilderment with practical certitude by approving even such limited cloning for experimental purposes.

Protestants are often pictured—erroneously in many respects—as stout defenders of human freedom. But whatever the accuracy of that depiction, they have not had in mind a freedom without limit, without even the limit that is God. They have not located the dignity of human beings in a self-modifying freedom that knows no limit and that need never respect a limit which it can, in principle, transgress. It is the meaning of the child—offspring of a man and woman, but a replication of neither; their offspring, but not their product whose meaning and destiny they might determine—that, I think, constitutes such a limit to our freedom to make and remake ourselves. In the face of that mystery I hope that your Commission will remember that "progress" is always an optional goal in which nothing of the sacred inheres.

5

Human Cloning Should Be Banned

Leon R. Kass

Leon R. Kass is Addie Clark Harding Professor at the College and the Committee on Social Thought at the University of Chicago.

The widespread use of reproductive technologies has led people to accept the possibility of human cloning as just another technological advance. Therefore, if human cloning research is permitted, it is likely that humans will be cloned. Most people naturally find the idea of human cloning repugnant, though many find it hard to logically justify this feeling. But human cloning would be unethical for three reasons: The genetic and social identity of the cloned person would be unclear; a cloned human would be a manufactured product inherently lower in status than those who made him or her; and parents would be in a controlling position above their cloned child. Since it is likely that cloning research on animals and human embryos will be permitted to proceed, it is necessary to establish an effective ban on research intended to produce a cloned human being.

Our habit of delighting in news of scientific and technological breakthroughs has been sorely challenged by the birth announcement of a sheep named Dolly. Though Dolly shares with previous sheep the "softest clothing, woolly, bright," William Blake's question, "Little Lamb, who made thee?" has for her a radically different answer: Dolly was, quite literally, made. She is the work not of nature or nature's God but of man, an Englishman, Ian Wilmut, and his fellow scientists. What's more, Dolly came into being not only asexually—ironically, just like "He [who] calls Himself a Lamb"—but also as the genetically identical copy (and the perfect incarnation of the form or blueprint) of a mature ewe, of whom she is a clone. This long-awaited yet not quite expected success in cloning a mammal raised immediately the prospect—and the specter—of cloning human beings: "I a child and Thou a lamb," despite our differences, have always been equal candidates for creative making, only now, by means of

From Leon R. Kass, "The Wisdom of Repugnance," *New Republic*, June 2, 1997. Reprinted by permission of the *New Republic*; ©1997, The New Republic, Inc.

cloning, we may both spring from the hand of man playing at being God.

After an initial flurry of expert comment and public consternation, with opinion polls showing overwhelming opposition to cloning human beings, President Clinton ordered a ban on all federal support for human cloning research (even though none was being supported) and charged the National Bioethics Advisory Commission to report in ninety days on the ethics of human cloning research. The commission (an eighteen-member panel, evenly balanced between scientists and nonscientists, appointed by the president and reporting to the National Science and Technology Council) invited testimony from scientists, religious thinkers and bioethicists, as well as from the general public. It is now deliberating about what it should recommend, both as a matter of ethics and as a matter of public policy.

Congress is awaiting the commission's report, and is poised to act. Bills to prohibit the use of federal funds for human cloning research have been introduced in the House of Representatives and the Senate; and another bill, in the House, would make it illegal "for any person to use a human somatic cell for the process of producing a human clone." A fateful decision is at hand. To clone or not to clone a human being is no longer an academic question.

Taking cloning seriously, then and now

Cloning first came to public attention roughly thirty years ago, following the successful asexual production, in England, of a clutch of tadpole clones by the technique of nuclear transplantation. The individual largely responsible for bringing the prospect and promise of human cloning to public notice was Joshua Lederberg, a Nobel Laureate geneticist and a man of large vision. In 1966, Lederberg wrote a remarkable article in *The American Naturalist* detailing the eugenic advantages of human cloning and other forms of genetic engineering, and the following year he devoted a column in *The Washington Post*, where he wrote regularly on science and society, to the prospect of human cloning. He suggested that cloning could help us overcome the unpredictable variety that still rules human reproduction, and allow us to benefit from perpetuating superior genetic endowments. These writings sparked a small public debate in which I became a participant. At the time a young researcher in molecular biology at the National Institutes of Health (NIH), I wrote a reply to the *Post*, arguing against Lederberg's amoral treatment of this morally weighty subject and insisting on the urgency of confronting a series of questions and objections, culminating in the suggestion that "the programmed reproduction of man will, in fact, dehumanize him."

Much has happened in the intervening years. It has become harder, not easier, to discern the true meaning of human cloning. We have in some sense been softened up to the idea—through movies, cartoons, jokes and intermittent commentary in the mass media, some serious, most lighthearted. We have become accustomed to new practices in human reproduction: not just in vitro fertilization, but also embryo manipulation, embryo donation and surrogate pregnancy. Animal biotechnology has yielded transgenic animals and a burgeoning science of genetic engineering, easily and soon to be transferable to humans.

Even more important, changes in the broader culture make it now vastly more difficult to express a common and respectful understanding of sexuality, procreation, nascent life, family, and the meaning of motherhood, fatherhood and the links between the generations. Twenty-five years ago, abortion was still largely illegal and thought to be immoral, the sexual revolution (made possible by the extramarital use of the pill) was still in its infancy, and few had yet heard about the reproductive rights of single women, homosexual men and lesbians. (Never mind shameless memoirs about one's own incest!) Then one could argue, without embarrassment, that the new technologies of human reproduction—babies without sex—and their confounding of normal kin relations—who's the mother: the egg donor, the surrogate who carries and delivers, or the one who rears?—would "undermine the justification and support that biological parenthood gives to the monogamous marriage." Today, defenders of stable, monogamous marriage risk charges of giving offense to those adults who are living in "new family forms" or to those children who, even without the benefit of assisted reproduction, have acquired either three or four parents or one or none at all. Today, one must even apologize for voicing opinions that twenty-five years ago were nearly universally regarded as the core of our culture's wisdom on these matters. In a world whose once-given natural boundaries are blurred by technological change and whose moral boundaries are seemingly up for grabs, it is much more difficult to make persuasive the still compelling case against cloning human beings. As Raskolnikov put it, "man gets used to everything—the beast!"

Cloning and postmodern culture

Indeed, perhaps the most depressing feature of the discussions that immediately followed the news about Dolly was their ironical tone, their genial cynicism, their moral fatigue: "An Udder Way of Making Lambs" (*Nature*), "Who Will Cash in on Breakthrough in Cloning?" (*The Wall Street Journal*), "Is Cloning Baaaaaaad?" (*The Chicago Tribune*). Gone from the scene are the wise and courageous voices of Theodosius Dobzhansky (genetics), Hans Jonas (philosophy) and Paul Ramsey (theology) who, only twenty-five years ago, all made powerful moral arguments against ever cloning a human being. We are now too sophisticated for such argumentation; we wouldn't be caught in public with a strong moral stance, never mind an absolutist one. We are all, or almost all, post-modernists now.

Cloning turns out to be the perfect embodiment of the ruling opinions of our new age. Thanks to the sexual revolution, we are able to deny in practice, and increasingly in thought, the inherent procreative teleology of sexuality itself. But, if sex has no intrinsic connection to generating babies, babies need have no necessary connection to sex. Thanks to feminism and the gay rights movement, we are increasingly encouraged to treat the natural heterosexual difference and its preeminence as a matter of "cultural construction." But if male and female are not normatively complementary and generatively significant, babies need not come from male and female complementarity. Thanks to the prominence and the acceptability of divorce and out-of-wedlock births, stable, monogamous marriage as the ideal home for procreation is no longer the agreed-upon cultural norm. For this new dispensation, the clone is the ideal emblem: the ultimate "single-parent child."

Thanks to our belief that all children should be *wanted* children (the more high-minded principle we use to justify contraception and abortion), sooner or later only those children who fulfill our wants will be fully acceptable. Through cloning, we can work our wants and wills on the very identity of our children, exercising control as never before. Thanks to modern notions of individualism and the rate of cultural change, we see ourselves not as linked to ancestors and defined by traditions, but as projects for our own self-creation, not only as self-made men but also man-made selves; and self-cloning is simply an extension of such rootless and narcissistic self-re-creation.

Ethicists have for the most part been content, after some "values clarification" and wringing of hands, to pronounce their blessings upon the inevitable.

Unwilling to acknowledge our debt to the past and unwilling to embrace the uncertainties and the limitations of the future, we have a false relation to both: cloning personifies our desire fully to control the future, while being subject to no controls ourselves. Enchanted and enslaved by the glamour of technology, we have lost our awe and wonder before the deep mysteries of nature and of life. We cheerfully take our own beginnings in our hands and, like the last man, we blink.

Part of the blame for our complacency lies, sadly, with the field of bioethics itself, and its claim to expertise in these moral matters. Bioethics was founded by people who understood that the new biology touched and threatened the deepest matters of our humanity: bodily integrity, identity and individuality, lineage and kinship, freedom and self-command, eros and aspiration, and the relations and strivings of body and soul. With its capture by analytic philosophy, however, and its inevitable routinization and professionalization, the field has by and large come to content itself with analyzing moral arguments, reacting to new technological developments and taking on emerging issues of public policy, all performed with a naïve faith that the evils we fear can all be avoided by compassion, regulation and a respect for autonomy. Bioethics has made some major contributions in the protection of human subjects and in other areas where personal freedom is threatened; but its practitioners, with few exceptions, have turned the big human questions into pretty thin gruel.

One reason for this is that the piecemeal formation of public policy tends to grind down large questions of morals into small questions of procedure. Many of the country's leading bioethicists have served on national commissions or state task forces and advisory boards, where, understandably, they have found utilitarianism to be the only ethical vocabulary acceptable to all participants in discussing issues of law, regulation and public policy. As many of these commissions have been either officially under the aegis of NIH or the Health and Human Services Department, or otherwise dominated by powerful voices for scientific progress, the ethicists have for the most part been content, after some "values clarification" and wringing of hands, to pronounce their blessings upon the inevitable. Indeed, it is the bioethicists, not the scientists, who are now the most articulate defenders of human cloning: the two witnesses testifying before the National Bioethics Advisory Commission [in March 1997] in favor of cloning human beings were bioethicists, eager to rebut what they regard as the irrational concerns of those of us in opposition. One wonders whether this commission, constituted like the previous commissions, can tear itself sufficiently free from the accommodationist pattern of rubber-stamping all technical innovation, in the mistaken belief that all other goods must bow down before the gods of better health and scientific advance.

If it is to do so, the commission must first persuade itself, as we all should persuade ourselves, not to be complacent about what is at issue here. Human cloning, though it is in some respects continuous with previous reproductive technologies, also represents something radically new, in itself and in its easily foreseeable consequences. The stakes are very high indeed. I exaggerate, but in the direction of the truth, when I insist that we are faced with having to decide nothing less than whether human procreation is going to remain human, whether children are going to be made rather than begotten, whether it is a good thing, humanly speaking, to say yes in principle to the road which leads (at best) to the dehumanized rationality of *Brave New World*. This is not business as usual, to be fretted about for a while but finally to be given our seal of approval. We must rise to the occasion and make our judgments as if the future of our humanity hangs in the balance. For so it does.

The state of the art

If we should not underestimate the significance of human cloning, neither should we exaggerate its imminence or misunderstand just what is involved. The procedure is conceptually simple. The nucleus of a mature but unfertilized egg is removed and replaced with a nucleus obtained from a specialized cell of an adult (or fetal) organism (in Dolly's case, the donor nucleus came from mammary gland epithelium). Since almost all the hereditary material of a cell is contained within its nucleus, the renucleated egg and the individual into which this egg develops are genetically identical to the organism that was the source of the transferred nucleus. An unlimited number of genetically identical individuals— clones— could be produced by nuclear transfer. In principle, any person, male or female, newborn or adult, could be cloned, and in any quantity. With laboratory cultivation and storage of tissues, cells outliving their sources make it possible even to clone the dead.

The technical stumbling block, overcome by Wilmut and his colleagues, was to find a means of reprogramming the state of the DNA in the donor cells, reversing its differentiated expression and restoring its full totipotency, so that it could again direct the entire process of producing a mature organism. Now that this problem has been solved, we should expect a rush to develop cloning for other animals, especially livestock, in order to propagate in perpetuity the champion meat or milk producers. Though exactly how soon someone will succeed in cloning a human being is anybody's guess, Wilmut's technique, almost certainly applicable to humans, makes *attempting* the feat an imminent possibility.

Yet some cautions are in order and some possible misconceptions need correcting. For a start, cloning is not Xeroxing. As has been reassuringly reiterated, the clone of Mel Gibson, though his genetic double, would enter the world hairless, toothless and peeing in his diapers, just like any other human infant. Moreover, the success rate, at least at first, will probably not be very high: the British transferred 277 adult nuclei into enucleated sheep eggs, and implanted twenty-nine clonal embryos, but they achieved the birth of only one live lamb clone. For this reason, among others, it is unlikely that, at least for now, the practice would be very popular, and there is no immediate worry of mass-scale production of multicopies. The need of repeated surgery to obtain eggs and, more crucially, of numerous borrowed wombs for implantation will surely limit use, as will the expense; besides, almost everyone who is able will doubtless prefer nature's sexier way of conceiving.

Though exactly how soon someone will succeed in cloning a human being is anybody's guess, Wilmut's technique . . . makes attempting *the feat an imminent possibility.*

Still, for the tens of thousands of people already sustaining over 200 assisted-reproduction clinics in the United States and already availing themselves of in vitro fertilization, intracytoplasmic sperm injection and other techniques of assisted reproduction, cloning would be an option with virtually no added fuss (especially when the success rate improves). Should commercial interests develop in "nucleus-banking," as they have in sperm-banking; should famous athletes or other celebrities decide to market their DNA the way they now market their autographs and just about everything else; should techniques of embryo and germline genetic testing and manipulation arrive as anticipated, increasing the use of laboratory assistance in order to obtain "better" babies—should all this come to pass, then cloning, if it is permitted, could become more than a marginal practice simply on the basis of free reproductive choice, even without any social encouragement to upgrade the gene pool or to replicate superior types. Moreover, if laboratory research on human cloning proceeds, even without any intention to produce cloned humans, the existence of cloned human embryos in the laboratory, created to begin with only for research purposes, would surely pave the way for later baby-making implantations.

In anticipation of human cloning, apologists and proponents have already made clear possible uses of the perfected technology, ranging from the sentimental and compassionate to the grandiose. They include: providing a child for an infertile couple; "replacing" a beloved spouse or child who is dying or has died; avoiding the risk of genetic disease; permitting reproduction for homosexual men and lesbians who want nothing sexual to do with the opposite sex; securing a genetically identical source of organs or tissues perfectly suitable for transplantation; getting a child with a genotype of one's own choosing, not excluding oneself; replicating individuals of great genius, talent or beauty—having a child who really could "be like Mike"; and creating large sets of genetically identical humans suitable for research on, for instance, the question of nature versus nurture, or for special missions in peace and war (not excluding espionage), in which using identical humans would be an advantage. Most people who envision the cloning of human beings, of course, want none of these scenarios. That they cannot say why is not surprising. What is surprising, and welcome, is that, in our cynical age, they are saying anything at all.

The wisdom of repugnance

"Offensive." "Grotesque." "Revolting." "Repugnant." "Repulsive." These are the words most commonly heard regarding the prospect of human cloning. Such reactions come both from the man or woman in the street and from the intellectuals, from believers and atheists, from humanists and scientists. Even Dolly's creator has said he "would find it offensive" to clone a human being.

People are repelled by many aspects of human cloning. They recoil from the prospect of mass production of human beings, with large clones of look-alikes, compromised in their individuality; the idea of father-son or mother-daughter twins; the bizarre prospects of a woman giving birth to and rearing a genetic copy of herself, her spouse or even her deceased father or mother; the grotesqueness of conceiving a child as an exact replacement for another who has died; the utilitarian creation of embryonic genetic duplicates of oneself, to be frozen away or created when necessary, in case of need for homologous tissues or organs for transplantation; the narcissism of those who would clone themselves and the arrogance of others who think they know who deserves to be cloned or which genotype any child-to-be should be thrilled to receive; the Frankensteinian hubris to create human life and increasingly to control its destiny; man playing God. Almost no one finds any of the suggested reasons for human cloning compelling; almost everyone anticipates its possible misuses and abuses. Moreover, many people feel oppressed by the sense that there is probably nothing we can do to prevent it from happening. This makes the prospect all the more revolting.

Revulsion is not an argument; and some of yesterday's repugnances are today calmly accepted—though, one must add, not always for the better. In crucial cases, however, repugnance is the emotional expression of deep wisdom, beyond reason's power fully to articulate it. Can anyone really give an argument fully adequate to the horror which is father-daughter incest (even with consent), or having sex with animals, or mutilating a corpse, or eating human flesh, or even just (just!) raping or murdering another human being? Would anybody's failure to give full rational justification for his or her revulsion at these practices make that revulsion ethically suspect? Not at all. On the contrary, we are suspicious of those who think that they can rationalize away our horror, say, by trying to explain the enormity of incest with arguments only about the genetic risks of inbreeding.

The repugnance at human cloning belongs in this category. We are repelled by the prospect of cloning human beings not because of the strangeness or novelty of the undertaking, but because we intuit and feel, immediately and without argument, the violation of things that we rightfully hold dear. Repugnance, here as elsewhere, revolts against the excesses of human willfulness, warning us not to transgress what is unspeakably profound. Indeed, in this age in which everything is held to be permissible so long as it is freely done, in which our given human nature no longer commands respect, in which our bodies are regarded as mere instruments of our autonomous rational wills, repugnance may be the only voice left that speaks up to defend the central core of our humanity. Shallow are the souls that have forgotten how to shudder.

The goods protected by repugnance are generally overlooked by our customary ways of approaching all new biomedical technologies. The way we evaluate cloning ethically will in fact be shaped by how we characterize it descriptively, by the context into which we place it, and by the perspective from which we view it. The first task for ethics is proper description. And here is where our failure begins.

Ethical perspectives on cloning

Typically, cloning is discussed in one or more of three familiar contexts, which one might call the technological, the liberal and the meliorist. Under the first, cloning will be seen as an extension of existing techniques for assisting reproduction and determining the genetic makeup of children. Like them, cloning is to be regarded as a neutral technique, with no inherent meaning or goodness, but subject to multiple uses, some good, some bad. The morality of cloning thus depends absolutely on the goodness or badness of the motives and intentions of the cloners: as one bioethicist defender of cloning puts it, "the ethics must be judged [only] by the way the parents nurture and rear their resulting child and whether they bestow the same love and affection on a child brought into existence by a technique of assisted reproduction as they would on a child born in the usual way."

The liberal (or libertarian or liberationist) perspective sets cloning in the context of rights, freedoms and personal empowerment. Cloning is just a new option for exercising an individual's right to reproduce or to have the kind of child that he or she wants. Alternatively, cloning enhances our liberation (especially women's liberation) from the confines of nature, the vagaries of chance, or the necessity for sexual mating. Indeed, it liberates women from the need for men altogether, for the process requires only eggs, nuclei and (for the time being) uteri—plus, of course, a healthy dose of our (allegedly "masculine") manipulative science that likes to do all these things to mother nature and nature's mothers. For those who hold this outlook, the only moral restraints on cloning are adequately informed consent and the avoidance of bodily harm. If no one is cloned without her consent, and if the clonant is not physically damaged, then the liberal conditions for licit, hence moral, conduct are met. Worries that go beyond violating the will or maiming the body are dismissed as "symbolic"—which is to say, unreal.

The meliorist perspective embraces valetudinarians and also eugenicists. The latter were formerly more vocal in these discussions, but they are now generally happy to see their goals advanced under the less threatening banners of freedom and technological growth. These people see in cloning a new prospect for improving human beings—minimally, by ensuring the perpetuation of healthy individuals by avoiding the risks of genetic disease inherent in the lottery of sex, and maximally, by producing "optimum babies," preserving outstanding genetic material, and (with the help of soon-to-come techniques for precise genetic engineering) enhancing inborn human capacities on many fronts. Here the morality of cloning as a means is justified solely by the excellence of the end, that is, by the outstanding traits or individuals cloned—beauty, or brawn, or brains.

These three approaches, all quintessentially American and all perfectly fine in their places, are sorely wanting as approaches to human procreation. It is, to say the least, grossly distorting to view the wondrous mysteries of birth, renewal and individuality, and the deep meaning of parent-child relations, largely through the lens of our reductive science and its potent technologies. Similarly, considering reproduction (and the intimate relations of family life!) primarily under the political-legal, adversarial and individualistic notion of rights can only undermine the private yet fundamentally social, cooperative and duty-laden character of child-bearing, child-rearing and their bond to the covenant of marriage. Seeking to escape entirely from nature (in order to satisfy a natural desire or a natural right to reproduce!) is self-contradictory in theory and self-alienating in practice. For we are erotic beings only because we are embodied beings, and not merely intellects and wills unfortunately imprisoned in our bodies. And, though health and fitness are clearly great goods, there is something deeply disquieting in looking on our prospective children as artful products perfectible by genetic engineering, increasingly held to our willfully imposed designs, specifications and margins of tolerable error.

> *We are repelled by the prospect of cloning human beings . . . because we intuit and feel . . . the violation of things that we rightfully hold dear.*

The technical, liberal and meliorist approaches all ignore the deeper anthropological, social and, indeed, ontological meanings of bringing forth new life. To this more fitting and profound point of view, cloning shows itself to be a major alteration, indeed, a major violation, of our given nature as embodied, gendered and engendering beings—and of the social relations built on this natural ground. Once this perspective is recognized, the ethical judgment on cloning can no longer be reduced to a matter of motives and intentions, rights and freedoms, benefits and harms, or even means and ends. It must be regarded primarily as a matter of meaning: Is cloning a fulfillment of human begetting and belonging? Or is cloning rather, as I contend, their pollution and perversion? To pollution and perversion, the fitting response can only be horror and revulsion; and conversely, generalized horror and revulsion are prima facie evidence of foulness and violation. The burden of moral argument must fall entirely on those who want to declare the widespread repugnances of humankind to be mere timidity or superstition.

Yet repugnance need not stand naked before the bar of reason. The wisdom of our horror at human cloning can be partially articulated, even if this is finally one of those instances about which the heart has its reasons that reason cannot entirely know.

The profundity of sex

To see cloning in its proper context, we must begin not, as I did before, with laboratory technique, but with the anthropology—natural and social—of sexual reproduction.

Sexual reproduction—by which I mean the generation of new life from (exactly) two complementary elements, one female, one male, (usually) through coitus—is established (if that is the right term) not by human decision, culture or tradition, but by nature; it is the natural way of all mammalian reproduction. By nature, each child has two complementary biological progenitors. Each child thus stems from and unites exactly two lineages. In natural generation, moreover, the precise genetic constitution of the resulting offspring is determined by a combination of nature and chance, not by human design: each human child shares the common natural human species genotype, each child is genetically (equally) kin to each (both) parent(s), yet each child is also genetically unique.

These biological truths about our origins foretell deep truths about our identity and about our human condition altogether. Every one of us is at once equally human, equally enmeshed in a particular familial nexus of origin, and equally individuated in our trajectory from birth to death—and, if all goes well, equally capable (despite our mortality) of participating, with a complementary other, in the very same renewal of such human possibility through procreation. Though less momentous than our common humanity, our genetic individuality is not humanly trivial. It shows itself forth in our distinctive appearance through which we are everywhere recognized; it is revealed in our "signature" marks of fingerprints and our self-recognizing immune system; it symbolizes and foreshadows exactly the unique, never-to-be-repeated character of each human life.

Human societies virtually everywhere have structured child-rearing responsibilities and systems of identity and relationship on the bases of these deep natural facts of begetting. The mysterious yet ubiquitous "love of one's own" is everywhere culturally exploited, to make sure that children are not just produced but well cared for and to create for everyone clear ties of meaning, belonging and obligation. But it is wrong to treat such naturally rooted social practices as mere cultural constructs (like left- or right-driving, or like burying or cremating the dead) that we can alter with little human cost. What would kinship be without its clear natural grounding? And what would identity be without kinship? We must resist those who have begun to refer to sexual reproduction as the "traditional method of reproduction," who would have us regard as merely traditional, and by implication arbitrary, what is in truth not only natural but most certainly profound.

Asexual reproduction, which produces "single-parent" offspring, is a radical departure from the natural human way, confounding all normal understandings of father, mother, sibling, grandparent, etc., and all moral relations tied thereto. It becomes even more of a radical departure when the resulting offspring is a clone derived not from an embryo, but from a mature adult to whom the clone would be an identical twin; and when the process occurs not by natural accident (as in natural twinning), but by deliberate human design and manipulation; and when the child's (or children's) genetic constitution is pre-selected by the parent(s) (or scientists). Accordingly, as we will see, cloning is vulnerable to three kinds of concerns and objections, related to these three points: cloning threatens confusion of identity and individuality, even in small-scale cloning; cloning represents a giant step (though not the first one) toward transforming procreation into manufacture, that is, toward the increasing depersonalization of the process of generation and, increasingly, toward the "production" of human children as artifacts, products of human will and design (what others have called the problem of "commodification" of new life); and cloning—like other forms of eugenic engineering of the next generation—represents a form of despotism of the cloners over the cloned, and thus (even in benevolent cases) represents a blatant violation of the inner meaning of parent-child relations, of what it means to have a child, of what it means to say "yes" to our own demise and "replacement."

Cloning represents a giant step (though not the first one) toward transforming procreation into manufacture.

Before turning to these specific ethical objections, let me test my claim of the profundity of the natural way by taking up a challenge recently posed by a friend. What if the given natural human way of reproduction were asexual, and we now had to deal with a new technological innovation—artificially induced sexual dimorphism and the fusing of complementary gametes—whose inventors argued that sexual reproduction promised all sorts of advantages, including hybrid vigor and the creation of greatly increased individuality? Would one then be forced to defend natural asexuality because it was natural? Could one claim that it carried deep human meaning?

The response to this challenge broaches the ontological meaning of sexual reproduction. For it is impossible, I submit, for there to have been human life—or even higher forms of animal life—in the absence of sexuality and sexual reproduction. We find asexual reproduction only in the lowest forms of life: bacteria, algae, fungi, some lower invertebrates. Sexuality brings with it a new and enriched relationship to the world. Only sexual animals can seek and find complementary others with whom to pursue a goal that transcends their own existence. For a sexual being, the world is no longer an indifferent and largely homogeneous *otherness*, in part edible, in part dangerous. It also contains some very special and related and complementary beings, of the same kind but of opposite sex, toward whom one reaches out with special interest and intensity. In higher birds and mammals, the outward gaze keeps a lookout not only for food and predators, but also for prospective mates; the beholding of the many splendored world is suffused with desire for union, the animal antecedent of human eros and the germ of sociality. Not by accident is the human animal both the sexiest animal—whose females do not go into heat but are receptive throughout the estrous cycle and whose males must therefore have greater sexual appetite and energy in order to reproduce successfully—and also the most aspiring, the most social, the most open and the most intelligent animal.

The soul-elevating power of sexuality is, at bottom, rooted in its strange connection to mortality, which it simultaneously accepts and tries to overcome. Asexual reproduction may be seen as a continuation of the activity of self-preservation. When one organism buds or divides to become two, the original being is (doubly) preserved, and nothing dies. Sexuality, by contrast, means perishability and serves replacement; the two that come together to generate one soon will die. Sexual desire, in human beings as in animals, thus serves an end that is partly hidden from, and finally at odds with, the self-serving individual. Whether we know it or not, when we are sexually active we are voting with our genitalia for our own demise. The salmon swimming upstream to spawn and die tell the universal story: sex is bound up with death, to which it holds a partial answer in procreation.

The salmon and the other animals evince this truth blindly. Only the human being can understand what it means. As we learn so powerfully from the story of the Garden of Eden, our humanization is coincident with sexual self-consciousness, with the recognition of our sexual nakedness and all that it implies: shame at our needy incompleteness, unruly self-division and finitude; awe before the eternal; hope in the self-transcending possibilities of children and a relationship to the divine. In the sexually self-conscious animal, sexual desire can become eros, lust can become love. Sexual desire humanly regarded is thus sublimated into erotic longing for wholeness, completion and immortality, which drives us knowingly into the embrace and its generative fruit—as well as into all the higher human possibilities of deed, speech and song.

> *Whether or not we know it, the severing of procreation from sex, love and intimacy is inherently dehumanizing, no matter how good the product.*

Through children, a good common to both husband and wife, male and female achieve some genuine unification (beyond the mere sexual "union," which fails to do so). The two become one through sharing generous (not needy) love for this third being as good. Flesh of their flesh, the child is the parents' own commingled being externalized, and given a separate and persisting existence. Unification is enhanced also by their commingled work of rearing. Providing an opening to the future beyond the grave, carrying not only our seed but also our names, our ways and our hopes that they will surpass us in goodness and happiness, children are a testament to the possibility of transcendence. Gender duality and sexual desire, which first draws our love upward and outside of ourselves, finally provide for the partial overcoming of the confinement and limitation of perishable embodiment altogether.

Human procreation, in sum, is not simply an activity of our rational wills. It is a more complete activity precisely because it engages us bodily, erotically and spiritually, as well as rationally. There is wisdom in the mystery of nature that has joined the pleasure of sex, the inarticulate longing for union, the communication of the loving embrace and the deep-seated and only partly articulate desire for children in the very activity by which we continue the chain of human existence and participate in the renewal of human possibility. Whether or not we know it, the severing of procreation from sex, love and intimacy is inherently dehumanizing, no matter how good the product.

We are now ready for the more specific objections to cloning.

The perversities of cloning

First, an important if formal objection: any attempt to clone a human being would constitute an unethical experiment upon the resulting child-to-be. As the animal experiments (frog and sheep) indicate, there are grave risks of mishaps and deformities. Moreover, because of what cloning means, one cannot presume a future cloned child's consent to be a clone, even a healthy one. Thus, ethically speaking, we cannot even get to know whether or not human cloning is feasible.

I understand, of course, the philosophical difficulty of trying to compare a life with defects against nonexistence. Several bioethicists, proud of their philosophical cleverness, use this conundrum to embarrass claims that one can injure a child in its conception, precisely because it is only thanks to that complained-of conception that the child is alive to complain. But common sense tells us that we have no reason to fear such philosophisms. For we surely know that people can harm and even maim children in the very act of conceiving them, say, by paternal transmission of the AIDS virus, maternal transmission of heroin dependence or, arguably, even by bringing them into being as bastards or with no capacity or willingness to look after them properly. And we believe that to do this intentionally, or even negligently, is inexcusable and clearly unethical.

The objection about the impossibility of presuming consent may even go beyond the obvious and sufficient point that a clonant, were he subsequently to be asked, could rightly resent having been made a clone. At issue are not just benefits and harms, but doubts about the very independence needed to give proper (even retroactive) consent, that is, not just the capacity to choose but the disposition and ability to choose freely and well. It is not at all clear to what extent a clone will truly be a moral agent. For, as we shall see, in the very fact of cloning, and of rearing him as a clone, his makers subvert the cloned child's independence, beginning with that aspect that comes from knowing that one was an unbidden surprise, a gift, to the world, rather than the designed result of someone's artful project.

Cloning distorts genetic identity

Cloning creates serious issues of identity and individuality. The cloned person may experience concerns about his distinctive identity not only because he will be in genotype and appearance identical to another human being, but, in this case, because he may also be twin to the person who is his "father" or "mother"—if one can still call them that. What would be the psychic burdens of being the "child" or "parent" of your twin? The cloned individual, moreover, will be saddled with a genotype that has already lived. He will not be fully a surprise to the world. People are likely always to compare his performances in life with that of his alter ego. True, his nurture and his circumstance in life will be different; genotype is not exactly destiny. Still, one must also expect parental and other efforts to shape this new life after the original—or at least to view the child with the original version always firmly in mind. Why else did they clone from the star basketball player, mathematician and beauty queen— or even dear old dad—in the first place?

Since the birth of Dolly, there has been a fair amount of doublespeak on this matter of genetic identity. Experts have rushed in to reassure the public that the clone would in no way be the same person, or have any confusions about his or her identity: as previously noted, they are pleased to point out that the clone of Mel Gibson would not be Mel Gibson. Fair enough. But one is shortchanging the truth by emphasizing the additional importance of the intrauterine environment, rearing and social setting: genotype obviously matters plenty. That, after all, is the only reason to clone, whether human beings or sheep. The odds that clones of Wilt Chamberlain will play in the NBA are, I submit, infinitely greater than they are for clones of Robert Reich.

Cloning radically confounds lineage and social relations, for "offspring" as for "parents."

Curiously, this conclusion is supported, inadvertently, by the one ethical sticking point insisted on by friends of cloning: no cloning without the donor's consent. Though an orthodox liberal objection, it is in fact quite puzzling when it comes from people (such as Ruth Macklin) who also insist that genotype is not identity or individuality, and who deny that a child could reasonably complain about being made a genetic copy. If the clone of Mel Gibson would not be Mel Gibson, why should Mel Gibson have grounds to object that someone had been made his clone? We already allow researchers to use blood and tissue samples for research purposes of no benefit to their sources: my falling hair, my expectorations, my urine and even my biopsied tissues are "not me" and not mine. Courts have held that the profit gained from uses to which scientists put my discarded tissues do not legally belong to me. Why, then, no cloning without consent—including, I assume, no cloning from the body of someone who just died? What harm is done the donor, if genotype is "not me"? Truth to tell, the only powerful justification for objecting is that genotype really does have something to do with identity, and everybody knows it. If not, on what basis could Michael Jordan object that someone cloned "him," say, from cells taken from a "lost" scraped-off piece of his skin? The insistence on donor consent unwittingly reveals the problem of identity in all cloning.

Genetic distinctiveness not only symbolizes the uniqueness of each human life and the independence of its parents that each human child rightfully attains. It can also be an important support for living a worthy and dignified life. Such arguments apply with great force to any large-scale replication of human individuals. But they are sufficient, in my view, to rebut even the first attempts to clone a human being. One must never forget that these are human beings upon whom our eugenic or merely playful fantasies are to be enacted.

Troubled psychic identity (distinctiveness), based on all-too-evident genetic identity (sameness), will be made much worse by the utter confusion of social identity and kinship ties. For, as already noted, cloning radically confounds lineage and social relations, for "offspring" as for "parents." As bioethicist James Nelson has pointed out, a female child cloned from her "mother" might develop a desire for a relationship to her "father," and might understandably seek out the father of her "mother," who is after all also her biological twin sister. Would "grandpa," who thought his paternal duties concluded, be pleased to discover that the clonant looked to him for paternal attention and support?

Social identity and social ties of relationship and responsibility are widely connected to, and supported by, biological kinship. Social taboos on incest (and adultery) everywhere serve to keep clear who is related to whom (and especially which child belongs to which parents), as well as to avoid confounding the social identity of parent-and-child (or brother-and-sister) with the social identity of lovers, spouses and co-parents. True, social identity is altered by adoption (but as a matter of the best interest of already living children: we do not deliberately produce children for adoption). True, artificial insemination and in vitro fertilization with donor sperm, or whole embryo donation, are in some way forms of "prenatal adoption"—a not altogether unproblematic practice. Even here, though, there is in each case (as in all sexual reproduction) a known male source of sperm and a known single female source of egg—a genetic father and a genetic mother—should anyone care to know (as adopted children often do) who is genetically related to whom.

> *Proponents want us to believe that there are legitimate uses of cloning that can be distinguished from illegitimate uses, but by their own principles no such limits can be found.*

In the case of cloning, however, there is but one "parent." The usually sad situation of the "single-parent child" is here deliberately planned, and with a vengeance. In the case of self-cloning, the "offspring" is, in addition, one's twin; and so the dreaded result of incest—to be parent to one's sibling—is here brought about deliberately, albeit without any act of coitus. Moreover, all other relationships will be confounded. What will father, grandfather, aunt, cousin, sister mean? Who will bear what ties and what burdens? What sort of social identity will someone have with one whole side—"father's" or "mother's"—necessarily excluded? It is no answer to say that our society, with its high incidence of divorce, remarriage, adoption, extramarital childbearing and the rest, already confounds lineage and confuses kinship and responsibility for children (and every-one else), unless one also wants to argue that this is, for children, a prefer-able state of affairs.

The differences between begetting and making children

Human cloning would also represent a giant step toward turning beget-ting into making, procreation into manufacture (literally, something "handmade"), a process already begun with in vitro fertilization and genetic testing of embryos. With cloning, not only is the process in hand, but the total genetic blueprint of the cloned individual is selected and determined by the human artisans. To be sure, subsequent development will take place according to natural processes; and the resulting children will still be recognizably human. But we here would be taking a major step into making man himself simply another one of the man-made things. Human nature becomes merely the last part of nature to succumb to the technological project, which turns all of nature into raw material at human disposal, to be homogenized by our rationalized technique according to the subjective prejudices of the day.

How does begetting differ from making? In natural procreation, human beings come together, complementarily male and female, to give existence to another being who is formed, exactly as we were, *by what we are:* living, hence perishable, hence aspiringly erotic, human beings. In clonal reproduction, by contrast, and in the more advanced forms of manufacture to which it leads, we give existence to a being not by what we are but by what we intend and design. As with any product of our making, no matter how excellent, the artificer stands above it, not as an equal but as a superior, transcending it by his will and creative prowess. Scientists who clone animals make it perfectly clear that they are engaged in instrumental making; the animals are, from the start, designed as means to serve rational human purposes. In human cloning, scientists and prospective "parents" would be adopting the same technocratic men-tality to human children: human children would be their artifacts.

Such an arrangement is profoundly dehumanizing, no matter how good the product. Mass-scale cloning of the same individual makes the point vividly; but the violation of human equality, freedom and dignity are present even in a single planned clone. And procreation dehumanized into manufacture is further degraded by commodification, a virtually inescapable result of allowing babymaking to proceed under the banner of commerce. Genetic and reproductive biotechnology companies are already growth industries, but they will go into commercial orbit once the Human Genome Project nears completion. Supply will create enormous demand. Even before the capacity for human cloning arrives, established companies will have invested in the harvesting of eggs from ovaries obtained at autopsy or through ovarian surgery, practiced embryonic genetic alteration, and initiated the stockpiling of prospective donor tis-sues. Through the rental of surrogate-womb services, and through the buy-ing and selling of tissues and embryos, priced according to the merit of the donor, the commodification of nascent human life will be unstoppable.

Finally, and perhaps most important, the practice of human cloning by nuclear transfer—like other anticipated forms of genetic engineering of the next generation—would enshrine and aggravate a profound and mischievous misunderstanding of the meaning of having children and of the parent-child relationship. When a couple now chooses to procreate, the partners are saying yes to the emergence of new life in its novelty, saying yes not only to having a child but also, tacitly, to having whatever child this child turns out to be. In accepting our finitude and opening ourselves to our replacement, we are tacitly confessing the limits of our control. In this ubiquitous way of nature, embracing the future by procreating means precisely that we are relinquishing our grip, in the very activity of taking up our own share in what we hope will be the immortality of human life and the human species. This means that our children are not *our* children: they are not our property, not our possessions. Neither are they supposed to live our lives for us, or anyone else's life but their own. To be sure, we seek to guide them on their way, imparting to them not just life but nurturing, love, and a way of life; to be sure, they bear our hopes that they will live fine and flourishing lives, enabling us in small measure to transcend our own limitations. Still, their genetic distinctiveness and independence are the natural foreshadowing of the deep truth that they have their own and never-before-enacted life to live. They are sprung from a past, but they take an uncharted course into the future.

Much harm is already done by parents who try to live vicariously through their children. Children are sometimes compelled to fulfill the broken dreams of unhappy parents; John Doe Jr. or the III is under the burden of having to live up to his forebear's name. Still, if most parents have hopes for their children, cloning parents will have expectations. In cloning, such overbearing parents take at the start a decisive step which contradicts the entire meaning of the open and forward-looking nature of parent-child relations. The child is given a genotype that has already lived, with full expectation that this blueprint of a past life ought to be controlling of the life that is to come. Cloning is inherently despotic, for it seeks to make one's children (or someone else's children) after one's own image (or an image of one's choosing) and their future according to one's will. In some cases, the despotism may be mild and benevolent. In other cases, it will be mischievous and downright tyrannical. But despotism—the control of another through one's will—it inevitably will be.

Meeting some objections

The defenders of cloning, of course, are not wittingly friends of despotism. Indeed, they regard themselves mainly as friends of freedom: the freedom of individuals to reproduce, the freedom of scientists and inventors to discover and devise and to foster "progress" in genetic knowledge and technique. They want large-scale cloning only for animals, but they wish to preserve cloning as a human option for exercising our "right to reproduce"—our right to have children, and children with "desirable genes." As law professor John Robertson points out, under our "right to reproduce" we already practice early forms of unnatural, artificial and extramarital reproduction, and we already practice early forms of eugenic choice. For this reason, he argues, cloning is no big deal.

We have here a perfect example of the logic of the slippery slope, and the slippery way in which it already works in this area. Only a few years ago, slippery slope arguments were used to oppose artificial insemination and in vitro fertilization using unrelated sperm donors. Principles used to justify these practices, it was said, will be used to justify more artificial and more eugenic practices, including cloning. Not so, the defenders retorted, since we can make the necessary distinctions. And now, without even a gesture at making the necessary distinctions, the continuity of practice is held by itself to be justificatory.

The principle of reproductive freedom as currently enunciated by the proponents of cloning logically embraces the ethical acceptability of sliding down the entire rest of the slope—to producing children ectogenetically from sperm to term (should it become feasible) and to producing children whose entire genetic makeup will be the product of parental eugenic planning and choice. If reproductive freedom means the right to have a child of one's own choosing, by whatever means, it knows and accepts no limits.

The so-called science fiction cases make vivid the meaning of what looks to us, mistakenly, to be benign.

But, far from being legitimated by a "right to reproduce," the emergence of techniques of assisted reproduction and genetic engineering should compel us to reconsider the meaning and limits of such a putative right. In truth, a "right to reproduce" has always been a peculiar and problematic notion. Rights generally belong to individuals, but this is a right which (before cloning) no one can exercise alone. Does the right then inhere only in couples? Only in married couples? Is it a (woman's) right to carry or deliver or a right (of one or more parents) to nurture and rear? Is it a right to have your own biological child? Is it a right only to attempt reproduction, or a right also to succeed? Is it a right to acquire the baby of one's choice?

The assertion of a negative "right to reproduce" certainly makes sense when it claims protection against state interference with procreative liberty, say, through a program of compulsory sterilization. But surely it cannot be the basis of a tort claim against nature, to be made good by technology, should free efforts at natural procreation fail. Some insist that the right to reproduce embraces also the right against state interference with the free use of all technological means to obtain a child. Yet such a position cannot be sustained: for reasons having to do with the means employed, any community may rightfully prohibit surrogate pregnancy, or polygamy, or the sale of babies to infertile couples, without violating anyone's basic human "right to reproduce." When the exercise of a previously innocuous freedom now involves or impinges on troublesome practices that the original freedom never was intended to reach, the general presumption of liberty needs to be reconsidered.

We do indeed already practice negative eugenic selection, through genetic screening and prenatal diagnosis. Yet our practices are governed by a norm of health. We seek to prevent the birth of children who suffer from known (serious) genetic diseases. When and if gene therapy becomes possible, such diseases could then be treated, in utero or even before implantation—I have no ethical objection in principle to such a practice (though I have some practical worries), precisely because it serves the medical goal of healing existing individuals. But therapy, to be therapy, implies not only an existing "patient." It also implies a norm of health. In this respect, even germline gene "therapy," though practiced not on a human being but on egg and sperm, is less radical than cloning, which is in no way therapeutic. But once one blurs the distinction between health promotion and genetic enhancement, between so-called negative and positive eugenics, one opens the door to all future eugenic designs. "To make sure that a child will be healthy and have good chances in life": this is Robertson's principle, and owing to its latter clause it is an utterly elastic principle, with no boundaries. Being over eight feet tall will likely produce some very good chances in life, and so will having the looks of Marilyn Monroe, and so will a genius-level intelligence.

Proponents want us to believe that there are legitimate uses of cloning that can be distinguished from illegitimate uses, but by their own principles no such limits can be found. (Nor could any such limits be enforced in practice.) Reproductive freedom, as they understand it, is governed solely by the subjective wishes of the parents-to-be (plus the avoidance of bodily harm to the child). The sentimentally appealing case of the childless married couple is, on these grounds, indistinguishable from the case of an individual (married or not) who would like to clone someone famous or talented, living or dead. Further, the principle here endorsed justifies not only cloning but, indeed, all future artificial attempts to create (manufacture) "perfect" babies.

Prudence dictates that one oppose . . . all production of cloned human embryos, even for research purposes.

A concrete example will show how, in practice no less than in principle, the so-called innocent case will merge with, or even turn into, the more troubling ones. In practice, the eager parents-to-be will necessarily be subject to the tyranny of expertise. Consider an infertile married couple, she lacking eggs or he lacking sperm, that wants a child of their (genetic) own, and propose to clone either husband or wife. The scientist-physician (who is also co-owner of the cloning company) points out the likely difficulties—a cloned child is not really their (genetic) child, but the child of only *one* of them; this imbalance may produce strains on the marriage; the child might suffer identity confusion; there is a risk of perpetuating the cause of sterility; and so on—and he also points out the advantages of choosing a donor nucleus. Far better than a child of their own would be a child of their own choosing. Touting his own expertise in selecting healthy and talented donors, the doctor presents the couple with his latest catalog containing the pictures, the health records and the accomplishments of his stable of cloning donors, samples of whose tissues are in his deep freeze. Why not, dearly beloved, a more perfect baby?

The "perfect baby," of course, is the project not of the infertility doctors, but of the eugenic scientists and their supporters. For them, the paramount right is not the so-called right to reproduce but what biologist Bentley Glass called, a quarter of a century ago, "the right of every child to be born with a sound physical and mental constitution, based on a sound genotype . . . the inalienable right to a sound heritage." But to secure this right, and to achieve the requisite quality control over new human life, human conception and gestation will need to be brought fully into the bright light of the laboratory, beneath which it can be fertilized, nourished, pruned, weeded, watched, inspected, prodded, pinched, cajoled, injected, tested, rated, graded, approved, stamped, wrapped, sealed and delivered. There is no other way to produce the perfect baby.

Yet we are urged by proponents of cloning to forget about the science fiction scenarios of laboratory manufacture and multiple-copied clones, and to focus only on the homely cases of infertile couples exercising their reproductive rights. But why, if the single cases are so innocent, should multiplying their performance be so off-putting? (Similarly, why do others object to people making money off this practice, if the practice itself is perfectly acceptable?) When we follow the sound ethical principle of universalizing our choice—"would it be right if everyone cloned a Wilt Chamberlain (with his consent, of course)? Would it be right if everyone decided to practice asexual reproduction?"—we discover what is wrong with these seemingly innocent cases. The so-called science fiction cases make vivid the meaning of what looks to us, mistakenly, to be benign.

Though I recognize certain continuities between cloning and, say, in vitro fertilization, I believe that cloning differs in essential and important ways. Yet those who disagree should be reminded that the "continuity" argument cuts both ways. Sometimes we establish bad precedents, and discover that they were bad only when we follow their inexorable logic to places we never meant to go. Can the defenders of cloning show us today how, on their principles, we will be able to see producing babies ("perfect babies") entirely in the laboratory or exercising full control over their genotypes (including so-called enhancement) as ethically different, in any essential way, from present forms of assisted reproduction? Or are they willing to admit, despite their attachment to the principle of continuity, that the complete obliteration of "mother" or "father," the complete depersonalization of procreation, the complete manufacture of human beings and the complete genetic control of one generation over the next would be ethically problematic and essentially different from current forms of assisted reproduction? If so, where and how will they draw the line, and why? I draw it at cloning, for all the reasons given.

Ban the cloning of humans

What, then, should we do? We should declare that human cloning is unethical in itself and dangerous in its likely consequences. In so doing, we shall have the backing of the overwhelming majority of our fellow Americans, and of the human race, and (I believe) of most practicing scientists. Next, we should do all that we can to prevent the cloning of human beings. We should do this by means of an international legal ban if possible, and by a unilateral national ban, at a minimum. Scientists may secretly undertake to violate such a law, but they will be deterred by not being able to stand up proudly to claim the credit for their technological bravado and success. Such a ban on clonal baby-making, more-over, will not harm the progress of basic genetic science and technology. On the contrary, it will reassure the public that scientists are happy to proceed without violating the deep ethical norms and intuitions of the human community.

This still leaves the vexed question about laboratory research using early embryonic human clones, specially created only for such research purposes, with no intention to implant them into a uterus. There is no question that such research holds great promise for gaining fundamental knowledge about normal (and abnormal) differentiation, and for devel-oping tissue lines for transplantation that might be used, say, in treating leukemia or in repairing brain or spinal cord injuries—to mention just a few of the conceivable benefits. Still, unrestricted clonal embryo research will surely make the production of living human clones much more like-ly. Once the genies put the cloned embryos into the bottles, who can strictly control where they go (especially in the absence of legal prohibi-tions against implanting them to produce a child)?

I appreciate the potentially great gains in scientific knowledge and medical treatment available from embryo research, especially with cloned embryos. At the same time, I have serious reservations about creating human embryos for the sole purpose of experimentation. There is some-thing deeply repugnant and fundamentally transgressive about such a utilitarian treatment of prospective human life. This total, shameless exploitation is worse, in my opinion, than the "mere" destruction of nascent life. But I see no added objections, as a matter of principle, to cre-ating and using *cloned* early embryos for research purposes, beyond the objections that I might raise to doing so with embryos produced sexually.

And yet, as a matter of policy and prudence, any opponent of the manufacture of cloned humans must, I think, in the end oppose also the creating of cloned human embryos. Frozen embryonic clones (belonging to whom?) can be shuttled around without detection. Commercial ven-tures in human cloning will be developed without adequate oversight. In order to build a fence around the law, prudence dictates that one oppose—for this reason alone—all production of cloned human embryos, even for research purposes. We should allow all cloning research on ani-mals to go forward, but the only safe trench that we can dig across the slippery slope, I suspect, is to insist on the inviolable distinction between animal and human cloning.

Some readers, and certainly most scientists, will not accept such pru-dent restraints, since they desire the benefits of research. They will prefer, even in fear and trembling, to allow human embryo cloning research to go forward.

Very well. Let us test them. If the scientists want to be taken serious-ly on ethical grounds, they must at the very least agree that embryonic research may proceed if and only if it is preceded by an absolute and effective ban on all attempts to implant into a uterus a cloned human embryo (cloned from an adult) to produce a living child. Absolutely no permission for the former without the latter.

The National Bioethics Advisory Commission's recommendations regarding this matter should be watched with the greatest care. Yielding to the wishes of the scientists, the commission will almost surely recommend that cloning human embryos for research be permitted. To allay public concern, it will likely also call for a temporary moratorium—not a legislative ban—on implanting cloned embryos to make a child, at least until such time as cloning techniques will have been perfected and rendered "safe" (precisely through the permitted research with cloned embryos). But the call for a moratorium rather than a legal ban would be a moral and a practical failure. Morally, this ethics commission would (at best) be waffling on the main ethical question, by refusing to declare the production of human clones unethical (or ethical). Practically, a moratorium on implantation cannot provide even the minimum protection needed to prevent the production of cloned humans.

Opponents of cloning need therefore to be vigilant. Indeed, no one should be willing even to consider a recommendation to allow the embryo research to proceed unless it is accompanied by a call for *prohibiting* implantation and until steps are taken to make such a prohibition effective.

Why a ban is necessary

Technically, the National Bioethics Advisory Commission can advise the president only on federal policy, especially federal funding policy. But given the seriousness of the matter at hand, and the grave public concern that goes beyond federal funding, the commission should take a broader view. (If it doesn't, Congress surely will.) Given that most assisted reproduction occurs in the private sector, it would be cowardly and insufficient for the commission to say, simply, "no federal funding" for such practices. It would be disingenuous to argue that we should allow federal funding so that we would then be able to regulate the practice; the private sector will not be bound by such regulations. Far better, for virtually everyone concerned, would be to distinguish between research on embryos and baby-making, and to call for a complete national and international ban (effected by legislation and treaty) of the latter, while allowing the former to proceed (at least in private laboratories).

The proposal for such a legislative ban is without American precedent, at least in technological matters, though the British and others have banned cloning of human beings, and we ourselves ban incest, polygamy and other forms of "reproductive freedom." Needless to say, working out the details of such a ban, especially a global one, would be tricky, what with the need to develop appropriate sanctions for violators. Perhaps such a ban will prove ineffective; perhaps it will eventually be shown to have been a mistake. But it would at least place the burden of practical proof where it belongs: on the proponents of this horror, requiring them to show very clearly what great social or medical good can be had only by the cloning of human beings.

We Americans have lived by, and prospered under, a rosy optimism about scientific and technological progress. The technological imperative—if it can be done, it must be done—has probably served us well, though we should admit that there is no accurate method for weighing benefits and harms. Even when, as in the cases of environmental pollution, urban decay or the lingering deaths that are the unintended by-products of medical success, we recognize the unwelcome outcomes of technological advance, we remain confident in our ability to fix all the "bad" consequences—usually by means of still newer and better technologies. How successful we can continue to be in such post hoc repairing is at least an open question. But there is very good reason for shifting the paradigm around, at least regarding those technological interventions into the human body and mind that will surely effect fundamental (and likely irreversible) changes in human nature, basic human relationships, and what it means to be a human being. Here we surely should not be willing to risk everything in the naïve hope that, should things go wrong, we can later set them right.

The president's call for a moratorium on human cloning has given us an important opportunity. In a truly unprecedented way, we can strike a blow for the human control of the technological project, for wisdom, prudence and human dignity. The prospect of human cloning, so repulsive to contemplate, is the occasion for deciding whether we shall be slaves of unregulated progress, and ultimately its artifacts, or whether we shall remain free human beings who guide our technique toward the enhancement of human dignity. If we are to seize the occasion, we must, as the late Paul Ramsey wrote,

> raise the ethical questions with a serious and not a frivolous conscience. A man of frivolous conscience announces that there are ethical quandaries ahead that we must urgently consider before the future catches up with us. By this he often means that we need to devise a new ethics that will provide the rationalization for doing in the future what men are bound to do because of new actions and interventions science will have made possible. In contrast a man of serious conscience means to say in raising urgent ethical questions that there may be some things that men should never do. The good things that men do can be made complete only by the things they refuse to do.

6

Animal Cloning Experiments Will Be Beneficial to Humans

Ian Wilmut, interviewed by Andrew Ross

Ian Wilmut is an embryologist and cloning researcher at the Roslin Institute in Scotland. Andrew Ross is managing editor of Salon, *a monthly on-line magazine.*

Human cloning research is ethically unacceptable due to the numbers of embryos that would be killed in such experiments. However, animal cloning research should be allowed because it can help scientists invent biomedical treatments for humans with serious diseases, produce organs for xenotransplantation (animal-to-human organ transplants), and create healthier, more disease-resistant livestock.

"Researchers Astounded . . . Fiction Becomes True and Dreaded Possibilities Are Raised." So went the headlines in Sunday's *New York Times* [February 23, 1997] about Dr. Ian Wilmut, the embryologist in Edinburgh who has made history by creating a lamb from the DNA of an adult sheep. The research, performed at the Roslin Institute in Edinburgh, was sponsored by a drug company, PPL Therapeutics.

Opening people's eyes

Dr. Wilmut says the primary purpose of the cloning is to advance the development of drug therapies to combat certain life-threatening human diseases. Other scientists, especially in the United States, appear to have adopted a more apocalyptic view of the news. "It basically means there are no limits," Dr. Lee Silver, a biologist at Princeton University, told the *New York Times.* "It means all of science fiction is true." Dr. Ronald Munson, a medical ethicist at the University of Missouri, said, "This technology is not, in principle, policeable." Munson even speculated about the possibility of cloning the dead.

From Ian Wilmut, "Dr. Frankenstein, I Presume?" an interview with Ian Wilmut by Andrew Ross, February 24, 1997. This article first appeared in *Salon,* an online magazine at http://www.salonmagazine.com. Reprinted with permission from *Salon.*

49

Are such scenarios remotely possible? And if drug treatment is the main priority, how soon will we see animal-clone-based drugs on the market? *Salon* spoke with Wilmut by telephone from his home in Edinburgh.

Andrew Ross: Science fiction. Cloning the dead. A technology out of control. What do you make of such reactions to your work?

Ian Wilmut: I think they're over the top. The point is that what we thought happens in all life is that you have a single fertilized egg and as it divides, it progressively differentiates and you get brain and muscle and all of the different kinds of cells that we have. People assumed until now that this was an irreversible process. And what we have shown is that it's not. Now people will have to think in slightly different ways about the mechanisms that control these changes—for example, about what happens when things go wrong and you get a cancer instead of a normal development. So it is going to open people's eyes a lot in terms of biology.

If there was a reason to copy a human being, we would do it, but there isn't.

And does it mean that cloning humans is possible?

We don't know. It is quite likely that it is possible, yes. But what we've said all along—speaking for both the (Roslin) Institute and the PPL staff—is that we would find it ethically unacceptable to think of doing that. We can't think of a reason to do it. If there was a reason to copy a human being, we would do it, but there isn't.

Is the idea of cloning the dead totally fanciful?

Yep.

Still, even if you can't clone the dead and you see no reason to clone the living, the genie is out of the bottle, so to speak. Others might find reasons for human cloning, and they may not have the same standard of ethics as you.

That does worry me, both in principle and in detail. It worries me in detail because the successes we have at present are of such low efficiency that it would really be quite appalling to think of doing that with people. I would feel desperately sorry for the women and the children that were involved.

Why? Because the clone could turn out to be some kind of monster?

It's possible. Perhaps you don't know that in the first experiment that we reported [in March 1996, in which sheep were cloned by nuclear transfer of embryonic cells], five lambs were born alive and three of them died quickly. There was nothing monstrous, they just simply died. That in itself is very distressing if you think of a mother who carries a child and it dies within a few days of birth.

The beneficial uses of animal cloning

Your main goal, you have said, is to develop health-related products from animal clones. In what areas, specifically?

Hemophilia. With animals, you could make the clotting factors which are missing. It could also be beneficial for cystic fibrosis.

What's the difference between using animal clones and other kinds of bio-technology techniques?

Speed and efficiency. You could take cells from an animal, grow them in the laboratory and make very precise genetic changes—it's called gene targeting—which you insert in the cloned offspring. So, for example, you put into the cells of the offspring DNA sequences which would say, "Don't make this particular milk protein, but instead make clotting factor 8," which is needed for hemophilia. You can do that now, but by using a much more primitive technique. Cloning and gene targeting requires fewer animals. It will be quicker, which means new health products will come on line more quickly.

There's another major advantage. Presuming this technique with sheep will successfully extend to cattle and then to pigs, it will speed xeno-transplantation—using organs from pigs to treat human patients. That can be done now, but what happens now is that you put a human protein into the pig organ which kind of damps down the immune response in the transplant patient. Now with gene targeting, we can do that, but we can also change the *surface* of the cells, so that they would be less antigenic when the pig organ is put into a human patient—which makes it more likely that organ transplantation will work.

History shows that people are very bad at predicting the way that technology will be used.

So, instead of waiting for a human donor, we'll be seeing many more animal-organ-to-human transplants.

Yes, with pig organs in particular.

And who would be helped the most?

Well, there is a need for more hearts and more kidneys. At present people die before human hearts can be made available to them.

There have been attempts to use baboon transplants in AIDS patients.

Yes, but people feel it's more acceptable to think of using pigs because baboons seem so much more—

—human?

That's right. Aware of their environment.

With animal cloning research, will it be possible to go in and fix genetic defects in humans? For example, there are already tests for a predisposition to breast cancer.

I think that is so far away that it's not really credible. I mean you're quite right theoretically. But the efficiencies we have at the present time and our understanding are so naive and primitive that you wouldn't con-template doing it. I think we could contribute in a smaller way to certain genetic diseases—breast cancer is not one that I've thought of—but, for example, with cystic fibrosis. It has been suggested that we study the role of the gene which is defective in people who suffer from cystic fibrosis with the hope that better therapies can be developed. We could also provide model test animals in which methods of gene therapy can be developed.

Which is being done with mice.

Yes, but mice are so different and so small that experimentation is very difficult. Sheep would be much more appropriate.

Do you see a therapy for cystic fibrosis based on animal clones in your lifetime?

Yes. I'm 52, I reckon I've got 20 years. I'm fairly comfortable predicting we'll see something in that time period.

The benefits of cloning for animals

In addition to drug therapy for humans, your research has major implications for animals.

Yes, it may open a whole range of things we can't imagine at the present time. Remember, we only know about what, 5 or 10 percent of the animal genes? But there is a particular project which is of immediate relevance in Britain concerning the disease scrapie.

Mad Cow Disease?

That's right. What people believe is that the agent which causes scrapie in sheep causes BSE (Bovine Spongiform Encephalitis) in cows and some of the CJD (Creuzfeld-Jacob Disease) in humans. It is believed to start with a particular gene in sheep. Now what if we could modify that gene; could we make sheep that are resistant to scrapie? That's very important for sheep, but also for BSE and CJD in humans.

When?

Twenty years or so.

There is also talk of "supercows" producing enormous quantities of milk. Could it be made cholesterol-free, by the way?

There are all sorts of questions like that. The answer to them is, we don't know. One thing I would say is that history shows that people are very bad at predicting the way that technology will be used.

Any implications for world hunger?

Not immediately. But if we can maybe make animals resistant to some diseases—to the tsetse fly, for example—it is quite possible that we can contribute to a whole range of things.

You've been working on this project for 10 years. Did you ever ask yourself, "Am I Dr. Frankenstein here? I know what I want to achieve but am I contributing to something I don't want to see happen?"

Of course. And we've tried to have this information released responsibly to journalists like yourself, to ethicists, to people concerned with legislation, because what we want is to stimulate an informed public discussion of the way in which the techniques might be misused as well as used and to ensure legislation was put in place to prevent misuse. But what we're also concerned with as well is that we don't throw the baby out with the bathwater. There are real potential benefits, and it's important that the concern to prevent misuse doesn't also prevent the really useful benefits that can be gained from this research.

What misuse are you most concerned with?

Any kind of manipulation with human embryos should be prohibited.

Are you concerned that your work will be stopped?

I have some concerns about it. I totally understand that people find this sort of research offensive, and I respect their views. It's also possible for a minority to have very large influence. Now, if society says it doesn't want us to do this kind of research, well, that's fine. But I think it has to be an overall view made by an informed population.

Assuming it goes forward, when will we see the first concrete applications?

I think there will be animals on the ground with interesting new products in three years. I think we'll come up with clotting factors, possibly in cattle as well as in sheep. Of course there will be a long time for testing the products before they go into commercial use. But there will be animals that are able to secrete new proteins, different proteins, in three years.

7

Animal Cloning May Be Acceptable Even If Human Cloning Is Unethical

Thomas H. Murray

Thomas H. Murray is director of the Center for Biomedical Ethics at Case Western Reserve University in Cleveland, Ohio, and a member of the National Bioethics Advisory Commission.

The cloning of an adult sheep is an incredible achievement, but many questions remain before this scientific advance will have practical benefits for humans. Ethical questions must be considered and addressed before human cloning research is permitted, but animal cloning research should not be banned.

Editor's note: The following remarks were presented as testimony to the U.S. House of Representatives Committee on Science, Subcommittee on Technology, on March 5, 1997, at a hearing titled "Biotechnology and the Ethics of Cloning: How Far Should We Go?"

I want to begin by thanking Representative Constance A. Morella, Chairwoman of this Subcommittee on Technology, for the invitation to speak with you today. Although I am not officially representing the National Bioethics Advisory Commission or its Chair, Dr. Harold Shapiro, of Princeton University, I believe I can fairly convey the Commission's gratitude for your interest in the subject of today's hearing, and our determination to make a full and timely response to the President's request for "a thorough review of the legal and ethical issues associated with the use of this technology," and for "recommendations on possible federal actions to prevent its abuse."

In that connection, it should be noted that Dr. Shapiro has already spurred the Commission into action on this issue, and that the bulk of the Commission's meeting scheduled for 13 and 14 March, 1997, will be

From Thomas H. Murray, testimony before the House Committee on Science, Subcommittee on Technology, March 5, 1997. (Subheadings and essay title added by Greenhaven Press.)

devoted to the issue of cloning. At that meeting we hope to hear a clear explanation of the science and potential applications of cloning. We are also calling upon leaders of the major religious traditions in the United States to present their views about the ethical issues raised by the prospect of cloning of human beings. We expect to have a frank and vigorous airing of concerns. As with all meetings of the Commission, there will also be time set aside for public testimony.

The need for facts

I want to speak now not as a member of a Presidential Commission or as a representative of my medical school or university, but as an ethicist, parent, and citizen with my own concerns about the possibility of human cloning. There is a saying in my field that "good ethics begins with good facts." The facts are just now emerging, so what I say today might have to be revised in the light of the better understanding of the facts that will come with time. The "facts" here include whether cloning of higher animals using the nuclear DNA of adults of that species can be accomplished efficiently, or whether Dolly was a fluke; whether the technology would work with humans; for what purposes people might want to clone humans.

We also need to see what laws we have in place now that are relevant to human cloning, as well as what current laws might be extended to cover it. It may well be that our laws governing research with human subjects could provide the protections that the American people believe are necessary.

If the techniques used to clone Dolly worked in humans, they could lend new meaning to the desire to "have a child just like myself." (Though, as one of my students reminded me, something very similar is occasionally uttered by frustrated parents when they say, "I hope you have a child just like yourself!") In any event, we have to cope with a new possibility—the conception and birth of genetic replicas of already existing persons.

We are all familiar with clones of a sort. Identical twins occur when one embryo divides into two genetically identical ones. If we applied cloning technology to ourselves we would be substituting controlled, intentional and perhaps decades-delayed cloning for the occasional accident of nature. But cloning strikes us as very different from the birth of identical twins. What is it about cloning that troubles us?

What cloning will not accomplish

It is important to understand what this new cloning technology cannot do. If someone were to clone a forty-year-old woman, you would not get another forty-year-old woman, but an embryo that would have to be implanted in a woman's uterus and pass through all of the normal stages of fetal development before birth. Then would come infancy, childhood and the throes of adolescence. It would be forty years and nine months before the cloned individual would be a forty-year-old woman herself— by which time the genetic source would be eighty or eighty-one. So, no instant copies.

I've spoken with many people recently about the possibility of cloning human beings. One suggested that if we were to ban human cloning, we should make an exception for Mel Gibson. I like Mel Gibson. The good news is that the clone may look a great deal like Mel Gibson. And that may be all that matters to some people. The bad news is that Mel's charm lies in his personality and wit at least as much as it does in his good looks. And Mel's clone could be very different from the original. He would have different parents, different friends, a lifetime of different experiences. He would come of age in a different historical era. The depression and world war shaped my parents' generation; mine came of age with rock and roll, and then Vietnam. My children's experience is different again from mine. Likewise with the cloned version of Mel Gibson. Our genes are merely the ground plan. Our personalities are made up as well by the totality of our life experiences, what we learn and whom we love. And no two lives are identical.

> *Our response to the possibility of human cloning should ask whether it supports or undermines what we value most about children and about being a parent.*

So why are we uneasy about cloning? We might be worried about the dangers of excessive control over human reproduction, about unbounded human pride. In the public debate that has begun, a great deal hinges on what questions we think are central. Some will want to ask, Who would be harmed by cloning? Whose rights would be violated? The claim that children are harmed by cloning requires comparing a possibly less-than-ideal existence with non-existence—a tough comparison to make. It's a bit like trying to divide by zero. In this case, you cannot get a very meaningful answer. Another appropriate question to ask is whose rights would be violated? Here we run into a similar problem as we did in trying to think about who is being harmed. If we are talking about violations of the child's rights, we encounter an interesting quandary. Until the child is created, there is no child whose rights we could violate, yet that creation would be accomplished by precisely those actions which we want to say violate the child's rights.

Neither of these arguments, it seems to me, reflect very well the depth of concern, indeed the revulsion, that many Americans feel in response to the prospect of cloning human beings. I share those concerns, and so I want to urge us to look for their strongest representations. Certainly, many people will reject cloning based on their religious beliefs. We will benefit from a vigorous and complete airing of those religious objections to human cloning.

I believe there are a set of moral concerns at the heart of our response to cloning that touch the most intimate and important relationships in our lives—the relationships of parents and children, the lives of families. I would like to see us begin by asking questions like What do we value most about the relationship of parents and children? What is it in the lives of families that we find most precious and worth preserving? Cloning, like other reproductive technologies, ought to be judged not just on whether it harms a particular person or violates someone's rights. Our response to the possibility of human cloning should ask whether it supports or undermines what we value most about children and about being a parent. In the realm of family life, choosing the precise genetic composition of your offspring (which is what cloning effectively does) may not be a virtue.

Last week I heard a man hail the idea of human cloning. He said that he looked forward to the prospect of cloning himself, then raising his child/himself without making all the mistakes his parents had made. I don't envy that child.

Responsible scientists will, I expect, have the same reaction to human cloning as Drs. Harold Varmus [director of the National Institutes of Health] and Ian Wilmut [of the Roslin Institute in Scotland, where the sheep was cloned], along with most non-scientists—that it is repugnant and should not be done. It is essential that we do our best to understand those moral objections and to give them their most cogent and forceful form.

It is also essential that we keep in view the possible scientific, and ultimately the human, benefits of research on animal cloning, benefits best described by the other witnesses before you today. It is important that our public policy response to research on the cloning of animals not be swept along by our concern to prevent what we will judge to be the ethical dangers of human cloning.

8

Cloning Can Be an Ethical Form of Human Reproduction

Alun M. Anderson

Alun M. Anderson is editor of New Scientist, *a weekly science magazine published in London.*

Though it is easy to imagine bizarre uses of cloning technology that resemble science fiction scenarios, it is also not difficult to think of beneficial uses for the new procedure. Cloning could assist infertile couples or those suffering from genetic diseases to have healthy children. Human cloning research should not be banned.

Dolly is surely the most remarkable animal ever born. She can't trace her parentage back to a ewe or a ram like every other sheep that has ever existed. Instead, she was artificially created by scientists in Scotland—grown from a single cell taken from the udder of an adult sheep. She is an identical clone of her "mother," if that is the right word for the donor sheep. And that makes her simultaneously both her mother's daughter and her identical twin sister.

Science fiction fears about cloning

We now have the power to take an adult sheep and replicate it endlessly. It is a truly awesome capability to contemplate. And since—biologically speaking—sheep aren't that different from humans, it probably wouldn't take much more research before we could create clones of humans too.

Should that research be allowed to take place? Should we obtain the power to clone human beings? Most people's first reaction is to say, "never." It seems so contrary to nature. And let's face it, the idea of cloning humans has always had a pretty bad press, starting back in 1932, when Aldous Huxley wrote *Brave New World*. In his fantasy of the future, sex has

From Alun M. Anderson, "Facing Science Fact—Not Fiction," *Washington Post*, March 12, 1997. Reprinted by permission of *New Scientist*.

become unnecessary and an all-powerful government clones an endless supply of human worker castes—the Gammas, Deltas and Epsilons.

The trouble with cloning is that it is all too easy to follow Huxley and dream up bizarre futuristic scenarios for its misuse. We can imagine worlds in which the rich and the powerful found dynasties in which they endlessly pass on their wealth to genetically identical but younger clones of themselves. Where the egotistical clone themselves so that they can give themselves the upbringing that they had always thought they deserved. Or where dictators perpetuate themselves for all time and clone their own fanatical guard of super-obedient soldiers. Fans of the famous might be able to indulge a ghoulish desire to bring their heroes back to life. How many seekers after Elvis might wish to see the King reborn—assuming that someone, somewhere, has a bit of frozen Elvis to clone from?

It's easy to find situations where it seems compassionate and ethical to allow the cloning of humans.

With speculation like this it's not surprising that many people believe that research on the cloning of humans should be banned. In Britain, where research has succeeded in creating Dolly, research on human cloning was prohibited back in 1990.

That was long before anyone thought it a possibility, and the decision now is hailed by some as remarkably farsighted and wise. Perhaps it wasn't. During the deliberations that led to the ban, little attempt was made to stimulate public debate on the ethics of cloning. As few people believed that the cloning of adult humans would be feasible, it didn't seem necessary. The law was framed simply to reflect popular sentiment: Cloning was the stuff of *Brave New World* and most likely impossible, so why not ban it?

The panel that has been asked by President Clinton to consider the ethics of cloning has no such excuse. The cloning of humans now looks all too possible. And when you put the wild speculations of science fiction writers out of your mind, it's easy to find situations where it seems compassionate and ethical to allow the cloning of humans.

Possible uses of human cloning

Take the case of a couple who have been to a genetic counselor and have found that they both carry a recessive gene for disease. It could be cystic fibrosis, for example, or sickle-cell anemia. The couple will know that if they have a child, they face a high risk that their child will suffer from the disease. Why, if cloning was safe, shouldn't one of them be given the opportunity to clone her or himself? They could be sure that the child would be healthy, and avoid prenatal testing and the subsequent agonizing decisions about whether or not to abort a baby afflicted by the genetic disease.

Would the public find it too strange for a mother to give birth to a daughter who is also her twin or a son who is the twin of her partner? It might not be that difficult an idea to get used to. After all, no one finds twins or even triplets too strange to deal with. Indeed, the nurture side of the equation would ensure that the cloned child would be less identical than identical twins who are brought up in the same environment at the same time—not a creepily exact replica of the parent à la *Brave New World*. Of course, the impact on the child's psychological development of knowing that he or she is a clone is still a great unknown.

How about the case of a woman who desperately wishes to have a child but finds herself infertile? Current choices are limited and already involve complicated medical procedures. The woman might be able to obtain an egg from a donor, have it fertilized in vitro with sperm from her partner and then implanted in her womb. The child's genetic makeup would be half that of another woman. Isn't a kinder—perhaps even more natural—alternative to allow the woman to give birth to a clone of herself?

In other, more tragic circumstances, cloning might provide some compassionate relief. Imagine a situation in which a woman finds her husband and newborn baby fatally injured in an automobile accident. Cloning could offer the opportunity to bring her baby back again.

The ability to construct human clones could benefit humankind.

These prospects are still unfamiliar and thus deeply disturbing. That does not mean they should not be contemplated. With an open debate, it is far from certain that everyone would object to every use of human cloning.

Once, artificial insemination was seen as so deeply abhorrent that its use was banned even for cattle. But the widespread public acceptance of test tube babies shows just how quickly new technologies can win hearts and grass-roots ethical approval when it touches upon the right to have a healthy child.

The Clinton committee should have the courage to discuss what the British government preferred to turn away from: that the ability to construct human clones could benefit humankind.

9

Cloning Should Not Be Banned Out of Fear

The Economist

The Economist *is a weekly magazine published in Britain.*

Calls to ban human cloning are based on unsubstantiated fears that cloning technology will be used for evil purposes. Technology is never bad in and of itself; it is the purposes for which it is used that can be malevolent. Though cloning research does present some dangers, it also has many potential benefits and should not be banned simply out of fear of its possible misuse.

Dolly is a lamb. As the first mammal to have been successfully "cloned" from the cells of an adult, she is the talk of the world. But what strange talk it has been. Bill Clinton declares himself troubled, and demands a report within 90 days. France's farm minister foresees hideous barnyard monstrosities: chickens with six legs and the like. The Vatican is aghast. Newspapers and pundits trundle out all the old fears and fantasies: armies of cloned Hitlers, Mozarts or Aldous Huxley's proletarian slaves.

Such fears are understandable. Even the godless find something repugnant in the idea that man might one day invent himself, instead of inventing his creator. But it is not enough merely to register repugnance, without examining the cause of this emotion and testing its claim against the claims of reason. To throw up one's hands in horror simply on the ground that cloning interferes with the natural order is to exaggerate the extent to which the natural order is desirable, and to under-estimate the extent to which man has already altered it, often with advantage.

First, though, some of the more outlandish worries need to be put in perspective. Science is probably a long way from being able to clone a human being. But what if it could? Much of this week's alarm stems from a confusion about what a clone would be. A clone is an organism that is genetically identical to another. Human clones already exist in the form of identical twins. But as anyone who has reared or met twins knows, they are not "identical" at all. Environment, experience and their own choices endow them with as much individuality as anyone else.

The spectre created by Dolly is that such twins might in future be parent and child instead of siblings; and that the younger is a twin on account of somebody's decision, rather than because of genetic accident. That is indeed a departure from the natural order of things, and may be a disturbing one, but it hardly justifies this outpouring of fear. Mozart's twin son would not necessarily be a brilliant musician even if he wanted to be, nor Hitler's a mass murderer. The narcissist who tried to copy himself by siring a twin would have no more control over this unusual relation than any other parent has over a normal child.

It is not enough merely to register repugnance, without examining the cause of this emotion and testing its claim against the claims of reason.

What about the prospect of eugenics, selective breeding and all that? Many people argue that in light of man's proven propensity to abuse powerful technologies (one Nobel laureate drew parallels with the nuclear bomb) it would be folly to put this new one into the hands of future dictators who may harbour mad dreams of master races or custom-bred slaves. But this argument is not only impractical (a tyrant would invent the technology if he wanted it); it is an argument against technology in general. The putative tyrant has no need of Dolly technology; he could already breed athletes as if they were racing horses, or pass a law forbidding short people to have babies. It is what people do that is good or bad, not what they can do. To put it another way, the fact that it would be wrong to force contraception on people is no argument against the continued existence of contraceptives.

Ban the clones?

Does all this mean that the possibility of human cloning should be joyously embraced? Far from it. It would be suicidal, not just dispiriting, for the species to give up sexual reproduction in favour of cloning. Sex creates new gene combinations that confer new strengths, especially resistance to disease. As a distinguished biologist, George C. Williams, put it many years ago, asexual reproduction is like xeroxing your lottery ticket; even if you have the winning number, making many copies won't help unless the winning number is the same every time. In the history of evolution asexual lineages of species have often appeared but few have lasted long.

This threat would not arise except in the unlikely event of a mass uptake of cloning. But there are ethical reasons why human cloning should not at present go ahead even in single cases. One is that the technology that produced Dolly is far from perfect. Even if it could be made to work in human cells, there are grounds to fear that a person produced in this way might age faster than normal, falling victim prematurely to the diseases of old age; or might turn out not to be fertile. It would be outrageous deliberately to create a person with such defects. But it is also hard to see how would-be cloners could ever be confident of their progeny being fully healthy without trying the technique out.

This Catch-22 may well stymie human cloning for ever. So why bother to dissent from the howl of protest that attended the advent of Dolly? Because it is an error to reach the right decision for the wrong reason. The vague feeling that cloning is an unnecessary offence against the natural scheme may very well solidify into a backlash against many of the other efforts of biologists. That would be a pity. Mankind has interfered with and reshaped the natural order for millennia. Agriculture, the domestication of animals and hunting have destroyed or altered more species and had more impact on the earth than Dolly is ever likely to have.

The fact that new technologies feel scary or strange should not be enough to rule them out. The careful application of biotechnology to plants and animals is already bringing benefits: better understanding of many diseases, new drug treatments, better health, to name a few. In genetics, in particular, medicine is poised to enter an age in which techniques such as gene therapy or genetic screening promise to add enormously to the sum of human well-being, even if they throw up complex ethical dilemmas on the way.

The dilemmas and risks need to be evaluated. To prevent unscrupulous businessmen or sinister scientists with dubious motives from conducting unethical experiments, rational debate followed by legislation is welcome-and necessary. But to turn away from what biology and medicine can do out of nostalgia for Eden would be folly indeed.

10

Human Cloning Has Not Been Proven Harmful

Ruth Macklin

Ruth Macklin is professor of bioethics at Albert Einstein College of Medicine in New York City.

Theologians and many others want human cloning banned because it might violate the human dignity and rights of those cloned. However, it is unlikely that cloned persons would be treated as less than human because it would be so clearly unethical to do so. On the contrary, human cloning research has many possible benefits and should therefore not be banned.

Last week's [February 23, 1997] news that scientists had cloned a sheep sent academics and the public into a panic at the prospect that humans might be next. That's an understandable reaction. Cloning is a radical challenge to the most fundamental laws of biology, so it's not unreasonable to be concerned that it might threaten human society and dignity. Yet much of the ethical opposition seems also to grow out of an unthinking disgust—a sort of "yuk factor." And that makes it hard for even trained scientists and ethicists to see the matter clearly. While human cloning might not offer great benefits to humanity, no one has yet made a persuasive case that it would do any real harm, either.

Theologians contend that to clone a human would violate human dignity. That would surely be true if a cloned individual were treated as a lesser being, with fewer rights or lower stature. But why suppose that cloned persons wouldn't share the same rights and dignity as the rest of us? A leading lawyer-ethicist has suggested that cloning would violate the "right to genetic identity." Where did he come up with such a right? It makes perfect sense to say that adult persons have a right not to be cloned without their voluntary, informed consent. But if such consent is given, whose "right" to genetic identity would be violated?

Many of the science-fiction scenarios prompted by the prospect of human cloning turn out, upon reflection, to be absurdly improbable. There's the fear, for instance, that parents might clone a child to have "spare parts" in case the original child needs an organ transplant. But parents of identical twins don't view one child as an organ farm for the other. Why should cloned children's parents be any different?

Vast difference. Another disturbing thought is that cloning will lead to efforts to breed individuals with genetic qualities perceived as exceptional (math geniuses, basketball players). Such ideas are repulsive, not only because of the "yuk factor" but also because of the horrors perpetrated by the Nazis in the name of eugenics. But there's a vast difference between "selective breeding" as practiced by totalitarian regimes (where the urge to propagate certain types of people leads to efforts to eradicate other types) and the immeasurably more benign forms already practiced in democratic societies (where, say, lawyers freely choose to marry other lawyers). Banks stocked with the frozen sperm of geniuses already exist. They haven't created a master race because only a tiny number of women have wanted to impregnate themselves this way. Why think it will be different if human cloning becomes available?

So who will likely take advantage of cloning? Perhaps a grieving couple whose child is dying. This might seem psychologically twisted. But a cloned child born to such dubious parents stands no greater or lesser chance of being loved, or rejected, or warped than a child normally conceived. Infertile couples are also likely to seek out cloning. That such couples have other options (in vitro fertilization or adoption) is not an argument for denying them the right to clone. Or consider an example raised by Judge Richard Posner: a couple in which the husband has some tragic genetic defect. Currently, if this couple wants a genetically related child, they have four not altogether pleasant options. They can reproduce naturally and risk passing on the disease to the child. They can go to a sperm bank and take a chance on unknown genes. They can try in vitro fertilization and dispose of any afflicted embryo—though that might be objectionable, too. Or they can get a male relative of the father to donate sperm, if such a relative exists. This is one case where even people unnerved by cloning might see it as not the worst option.

While human cloning might not offer great benefits to humanity, no one has yet made a persuasive case that it would do any real harm, either.

Even if human cloning offers no obvious benefits to humanity, why ban it? In a democratic society we don't usually pass laws outlawing something before there is actual or probable evidence of harm. A moratorium on further research into human cloning might make sense, in order to consider calmly the grave questions it raises. If the moratorium is then lifted, human cloning should remain a research activity for an extended period. And if it is ever attempted, it should—and no doubt will—take place only with careful scrutiny and layers of legal oversight. Most important, human cloning should be governed by the same laws that now protect human rights. A world not safe for cloned humans would be a world not safe for the rest of us.

11

Ethical Concerns About Cloning Are Misplaced

Robert Wachbroit

Robert Wachbroit is a research scholar at the Institute for Philosophy and Public Policy at the University of Maryland School of Public Affairs.

Many people incorrectly believe that cloning would produce children who are genetically predetermined to possess particular traits or to serve a utilitarian purpose and who consequently would be viewed as something less than human. Cloned humans would develop individually, the same as any other human, and therefore would be afforded the same rights as noncloned humans. A ban on human cloning would be counterproductive because it would encourage belief in genetic determinism—the false theory that an individual's personality is entirely determined by genes and that the environment plays no role in development. Such a ban also would likely be ineffective because cloning technology is simple to replicate, allowing research to be conducted in secret.

The news of the successful cloning of an adult sheep—in which the sheep's DNA was inserted into an unfertilized sheep egg to produce a lamb with identical DNA—has generated an outpouring of ethical concerns. These concerns are not about Dolly, the now famous sheep, nor even about the considerable impact cloning may have on the animal breeding industry, but rather about the possibility of cloning humans. For the most part, however, the ethical concerns being raised are exaggerated and misplaced, because they are based on erroneous views about what genes are and what they can do. The danger, therefore, lies not in the power of the technology, but in the misunderstanding of its significance.

Genetic determinism

Producing a clone of a human being would not amount to creating a "carbon copy"—an automaton of the sort familiar from science fiction. It would be more like producing a delayed identical twin. And just as iden-

From Robert Wachbroit, "To Clone or Not to Clone: That's the Question," *Washington Post National Weekly Edition*, March 10, 1997. Reprinted by permission of the author.

tical twins are two separate people—biologically, psychologically, morally and legally, though not genetically—so a clone is a separate person
from his or her non-contemporaneous twin. To think otherwise is to
embrace a belief in genetic determinism—the view that genes determine
everything about us, and that environmental factors or the random
events in human development are utterly insignificant. The overwhelming consensus among geneticists is that genetic determinism is false.

As geneticists have come to understand the ways in which genes
operate, they have also become aware of the myriad ways in which the
environment affects their "expression." The genetic contribution to the
simplest physical traits, such as height and hair color, is significantly
mediated by environmental factors. And the genetic contribution to the
traits we value most deeply, from intelligence to compassion, is conceded
by even the most enthusiastic genetic researchers to be limited and indi-
rect. Indeed, we need only appeal to our ordinary experience with identical twins—that they are different people despite their similarities—to
appreciate that genetic determinism is false.

Furthermore, because of the extra steps involved, cloning will probably always be riskier—that is, less likely to result in a live birth—than in
vitro fertilization (IVF) and embryo transfer. (It took more than 275
attempts before the researchers were able to obtain a successful sheep
clone. While cloning methods may improve, we should note that even
standard IVF techniques typically have a success rate of less than 20 percent.) So why would anyone go to the trouble of cloning?

Hypothetical uses of cloning and ethical considerations

There are, of course, a few reasons people might go to the trouble, and so
it's worth pondering what they think they might accomplish, and what
sort of ethical quandaries they might engender. Consider the hypotheti-
cal example of the couple who wants to replace a child who has died. The
couple doesn't seek to have another child the ordinary way because they
feel that cloning would enable them to reproduce, as it were, the lost
child. But the unavoidable truth is that they would be producing an
entirely different person, a delayed identical twin of that child. Once they
understood that it is unlikely they would persist.

But suppose they were to persist? Of course we can't deny that possibility. But a couple so persistent in refusing to acknowledge the genetic facts is not likely to be daunted by ethical considerations or legal
restrictions either. If our fear is that there could be many couples with
that sort of psychology, then we have a great deal more than cloning to
worry about.

Another disturbing possibility is the person who wants a clone in
order to have acceptable "spare parts" in case he or she needs an organ
transplant later in life. But regardless of the reason that someone has a
clone produced, the result would nevertheless be a human being with all
the rights and protections that accompany that status. It truly would be
a disaster if the results of human cloning were seen as less than fully
human. But there is certainly no moral justification for and little social
danger of that happening; after all, we do not accord lesser status to children who have been created through IVF or embryo transfer.

There are other possibilities we could spin out. Suppose a couple wants a "designer child"—a clone of Cindy Crawford or Elizabeth Taylor—because they want a daughter who will grow up to be as attractive as those women. Indeed, suppose someone wants a clone, never mind of whom, simply to enjoy the notoriety of having one. We cannot rule out such cases as impossible. Some people produce children for all sorts of frivolous or contemptible reasons. But we must remember that cloning is not as easy as going to a video store or as engaging as the traditional way of making babies. Given the physical and emotional burdens that cloning would involve, it is likely that such cases would be exceedingly rare.

A ban might encourage people to believe that there is a scientific basis for some of the popular fears associated with human cloning.

But if that is so, why object to a ban on human cloning? What is wrong with placing a legal barrier in the path of those with desires perverse enough or delusions recalcitrant enough to seek cloning despite its limited potential and formidable costs? For one thing, these are just the people that a legal ban would be least likely to deter. But more important, a legal barrier might well make cloning appear more promising than it is to a much larger group of people.

If there were significant interest in applying this technology to human beings, it would indicate a failure to educate people that genetic determinism is profoundly mistaken. Under those circumstances as well, however, a ban on human cloning would not only be ineffective but also most likely counterproductive. Ineffective because, as others have pointed out, the technology does not seem to require sophisticated and highly visible laboratory facilities; cloning could easily go underground. Counterproductive because a ban might encourage people to believe that there is a scientific basis for some of the popular fears associated with human cloning—that there is something to genetic determinism after all.

There is a consensus among both geneticists and those writing on ethical, legal and social aspects of genetic research, that genetic determinism is not only false, but pernicious; it invokes memories of pseudo-scientific racist and eugenic programs premised on the belief that what we value in people is entirely dependent on their genetic endowment or the color of their skin. Though most members of our society now eschew racial determinism, our culture still assumes that genes contain a person's destiny. It would be unfortunate if, by treating cloning as a terribly dangerous technology, we encouraged this cultural myth, even as we intrude on the broad freedom our society grants people regarding reproduction.

We should remember that most of us believe people should be allowed to decide with whom to reproduce, when to reproduce and how many children they should have. We do not criticize a woman who takes a fertility drug so that she can influence when she has children—or even how many. Why, then, would we object if a woman decides to give birth to a child who is, in effect, a non-contemporaneous identical twin of someone else?

By arguing against a ban, I am not claiming that there are no serious ethical concerns to the manipulation of human genes. Indeed there are. For example, if it turned out that certain desirable traits regarding intellectual abilities or character could be realized through the manipulation of human genes, which of these enhancements, if any, should be available?

But such questions are about genetic engineering, which is a different issue than cloning. Cloning is a crude method of trait selection: It simply takes a preexisting, unengineered genetic combination of traits and replicates it.

I do not wish to dismiss the ethical concerns people have raised regarding the broad range of assisted reproductive technologies. But we should acknowledge that those concerns will not be resolved by any determination we make regarding the specific acceptability of cloning.

12

Human Cloning
Is Inevitable

Rudy Baum

Rudy Baum is managing editor of Chemical & Engineering News, *a weekly science magazine.*

The technology that resulted in the cloning of a sheep will inevitably be applied to human beings. Though there are ethical concerns involved with human cloning, it is unlikely that this science will be used for evil purposes. Human and animal cloning research will produce useful scientific and biomedical discoveries and therefore should not be banned.

Ten days after the announcement that Scottish scientists had cloned an adult sheep—the first time an adult mammal had been cloned—President Clinton declared a ban in the U.S. on research aimed at cloning humans. In Congress, legislation was introduced to ban funding of such research and to make cloning humans a federal crime.

Fears about human cloning

The response of most politicians and journalists to the startling news from a lab near Edinburgh highlights the emptiness of what passes for public discourse today. For while cloning a sheep raises important public policy questions, mainly in the realm of animal husbandry, the primary topic politicians and journalists focused on was the possibility of cloning humans. You could almost hear the sonorous tones of doomsday prophets as you read their cautions against "playing God."

Then again, you could also hear the sounds of plain old hysteria. Reuters quoted Richard S. Nicholson, editor of the *Bulletin of Medical Ethics,* as saying, "The problem with all these new scientific techniques is once you've published it in an international journal like *Nature,* then it's available to any scientists regardless of how careful they are to practice within moral bounds around the world." He said that, in the U.K., "we are probably fairly safe from the Frankenstein factor, but the problem is

From Rudy Baum, "Playing God." Reprinted with permission from *Chemical Engineering News*, March 24, 1997, vol. 75, no. 12, p. 47. Copyright 1997 American Chemical Society.

that worldwide we certainly are not."

French Minister for Agriculture, Fisheries & Food Philippe Vasseur, according to Reuters, worried about someone inventing "sheep with eight feet or chickens with six legs." There's a scary thought.

Let's be clear about this: Cloning a human with the goal of creating a carbon copy of an existing adult is a notion fraught with profound moral dilemmas. But almost nobody in his right mind wants to do that.

Whether it will be possible to clone humans remains unknown, of course. No one knows whether Dolly, the cloned sheep, is an anomaly. Cloning mammals may turn out to be incredibly difficult, or it may turn out to be quite simple. If it is simple, it will be difficult to police. At a hearing of the Technology Subcommittee of the House Science Committee held shortly after the announcement of the breakthrough, witnesses conceded that setting up a facility to clone humans would probably cost no more than $100,000 and involve readily available equipment.

Uses of cloning in animal husbandry

What scientists eventually want to do with animals such as sheep and cattle is to use genetic engineering to introduce a desirable trait into an animal. Given the current state of genetic engineering technology, that's still a hit-or-miss proposition, with far more misses than hits. What cloning will allow, if it proves to be amenable to large-scale use, is the facile reproduction of a particularly good hit—an animal that optimally expresses a desired genetic trait—into a herd of animals that express that trait.

There are serious issues about such an approach to animal husbandry that need to be addressed, primarily involving the potential loss of genetic diversity among domestic farm animals and the resulting susceptibility to catastrophic disease. But they are extensions of issues that are already well known.

And contrary to the instantaneous conventional wisdom, there are good reasons to want to clone adult human cells, not to produce Frankensteins, but to understand the profoundly complex and important process of cell differentiation. That's the process that allows a fertilized egg to develop into a complete organism. That's the process that, when it is partially unhinged, leads to cancer.

Now we've learned how to clone animals and, probably, people. It's all part of a continuum, a technological imperative that is as unstoppable as the passage of time.

While we want to understand cell differentiation in general, we want to understand it in humans in particular. Cloning adult human cells and observing their subsequent development could make an important contribution to such research. It makes a lot more sense to study these processes in human cells than it does to study them in animal cells and try to extrapolate the results to humans. You don't have to create a fully developed human to carry out such research.

But back to the Frankenstein problem: If the Scottish results can be reproduced and prove to be extendible to humans, will some astronomically rich, egomaniacal superstar or some deranged, egomaniacal dictator try to clone him- or herself? Of course. To my mind, it is now a near certainty that someone, somewhere will have themselves cloned in the next 10 years. The procedure developed by Ian Wilmut and coworkers at the Roslin Institute just isn't that difficult to carry out, and the temptation is simply too great. That moral Rubicon has already been crossed.

Is that a moral catastrophe for humans? No. Is it the mark of our ultimate hubris, our need to "play God"? Certainly.

Playing God is what humans do for a living. We've been doing it for centuries. We rearranged the natural landscape through plant and animal breeding. We discovered vaccination and antibiotics to defeat plagues that once decimated populations. We exterminated species because they were in our way. We created reproductive technologies to aid people who would otherwise not be able to have children. We invented recombinant DNA technology to manipulate the genomes of organisms in whatever unnatural fashion suits our purposes. Now we've learned how to clone animals and, probably, people. It's all part of a continuum, a technological imperative that is as unstoppable as the passage of time. Humans playing God isn't always pretty and sometimes probably isn't even defensible, but moral outrage at this juncture strikes me as disingenuous given the history of human meddling in the biosphere, broadly defined to include ourselves.

Will humans use cloning wisely? Not always, but for the most part, I think they will. The vast majority of us don't want to create carbon copies of ourselves. That alone makes bans on human cloning research unnecessary and counterproductive.

13

Human Cloning Experiments Should Be Allowed

Ronald Bailey

Ronald Bailey is a contributing editor of Reason, *a monthly magazine of politics and economics.*

The news that scientists had successfully cloned an adult sheep prompted many premature calls to ban human cloning. There is no ethical reason to ban research aimed at human cloning. The fear that cloning will be used to produce second-class human beings is unfounded because cloning simply will not become widespread.

By now everyone knows that Scottish biotechnologists have cloned a sheep. They took a cell from a 6-year-old sheep, added its genes to a hollowed-out egg from another sheep, and placed it in the womb of yet another sheep, resulting in the birth of an identical twin sheep that is six years younger than its sister. This event was quickly followed up by the announcement that some Oregon scientists had cloned monkeys. The researchers say that in principle it should be possible to clone humans. That prospect has apparently frightened a lot of people, and quite a few of them are calling for regulators to ban cloning since we cannot predict what the consequences of it will be.

The rush to ban cloning

President Clinton rushed to ban federal funding of human cloning research and asked privately funded researchers to stop such research at least until the National Bioethics Advisory Commission issues a report on the ethical implications of human cloning. The commission, composed of scientists, lawyers, and ethicists, was appointed in 1996 to advise the federal government on the ethical questions posed by biotechnology research and new medical therapies. Its report is now due in June 1997.

From Ronald Bailey, "The Twin Paradox," *Reason*, May 1997. Reprinted with permission of the Reason Foundation, Los Angeles, California.

73

[In June 1997, the commission recommended that the moratorium on human cloning research be continued for three to five years—ed.]

But Sen. Christopher Bond (R-Mo.) isn't waiting around for the commission's recommendations; he's already made up his mind. Bond introduced a bill to ban the federal funding of human cloning or human cloning research. "I want to send a clear signal," said the senator, "that this is something we cannot and should not tolerate. This type of research on humans is morally reprehensible."

Carl Feldbaum, president of the Biotechnology Industry Organization, hurriedly said that human cloning should be immediately banned. Perennial Luddite Jeremy Rifkin grandly pronounced that cloning "throws every convention, every historical tradition, up for grabs." At the putative opposite end of the political spectrum, conservative columnist George Will chimed in: "What if the great given—a human being is a product of the union of a man and woman—is no longer a given?"

In addition to these pundits and politicians, a whole raft of bioethicists declared that they, too, oppose human cloning. Daniel Callahan of the Hastings Center said flat out: "The message must be simple and decisive: The human species doesn't need cloning." George Annas of Boston University agreed: "Most people who have thought about this believe it is not a reasonable use and should not be allowed. . . . This is not a case of scientific freedom vs. the regulators."

What exactly is wrong with it? Which ethical principle does cloning violate?

Given all of the brouhaha, you'd think it was crystal clear why cloning humans is unethical. But what exactly is wrong with it? Which ethical principle does cloning violate? Stealing? Lying? Coveting? Murdering? What? Most of the arguments against cloning amount to little more than a reformulation of the old familiar refrain of Luddites everywhere: "If God had meant for man to fly, he would have given us wings. And if God had meant for man to clone, he would have given us spores." Ethical reasoning requires more than that.

What would a clone be? Well, he or she would be a complete human being who happens to share the same genes with another person. Today, we call such people identical twins. To my knowledge no one has argued that twins are immoral. Of course, cloned twins would not be the same age. But it is hard to see why this age difference might present an ethical problem—or give clones a different moral status.

"You should treat all clones like you would treat all monozygous [identical] twins or triplets,"concludes Dr. H. Tristam Engelhardt, a professor of medicine at Baylor and a philosopher at Rice University. "That's it." It would be unethical to treat a human clone as anything other than a human being. If this principle is observed, he argues, all the other "ethical" problems for a secular society essentially disappear. John Fletcher, a professor of biomedical ethics in the medical school at the University of Virginia, agrees: "I don't believe that there is any intrinsic reason why cloning should not be done."

Let's take a look at a few of the scenarios that opponents of human cloning have sketched out. Some argue that clones would undermine the uniqueness of each human being. "Can individuality, identity and dignity be severed from genetic distinctiveness, and from belief in a person's open future?" asks George Will.

Will and others have apparently fallen under the sway of what Fletcher calls "genetic essentialism." Fletcher says polls indicate that some 30 percent to 40 percent of Americans are genetic essentialists, who believe that genes almost completely determine who a person is. But a person who is a clone would live in a very different world from that of his genetic predecessor. With greatly divergent experiences, their brains would be wired differently. After all, even twins who grow up together are separate people—distinct individuals with different personalities and certainly no lack of Will's "individuality, identity and dignity."

In addition, a clone that grew from one person's DNA inserted in another person's host egg would pick up "maternal factors" from the proteins in that egg, altering its development. Physiological differences between the womb of the original and host mothers could also affect the clone's development. In no sense, therefore, would or could a clone be a "carbon copy" of his or her predecessor.

What about a rich jerk who is so narcissistic that he wants to clone himself so that he can give all his wealth to himself? First, he will fail. His clone is simply not the same person that he is. The clone may be a jerk too, but he will be his own individual jerk. Nor is Jerk Sr.'s action unprecedented. Today, rich people, and regular people too, make an effort to pass along some wealth to their children when they die. People will their estates to their children not only because they are connected by bonds of love but also because they have genetic ties. The principle is no different for clones.

Horrifying cloning scenarios are exaggerations

Senator Bond and others worry about a gory scenario in which clones would be created to provide spare parts, such as organs that would not be rejected by the predecessor's immune system. "The creation of a human being should not be for spare parts or as a replacement," says Bond. I agree. The simple response to this scenario is: Clones are people. You must treat them like people. We don't forcibly take organs from one twin and give them to the other. Why would we do that in the case of clones?

The technology of cloning may well allow biotechnologists to develop animals which will grow human-compatible organs for transplant. Cloning is likely to be first used to create animals that produce valuable therapeutic hormones, enzymes, and proteins.

But what about cloning exceptional human beings? George Will put it this way: "Suppose a cloned Michael Jordan, age 8, preferred violin to basketball? Is it imaginable? If so, would it be tolerable to the cloner?" Yes, it is imaginable, and the cloner would just have to put up with violin recitals. Kids are not commercial property—slavery was abolished some time ago. We all know about Little League fathers and stage mothers who push their kids, but given the stubborn nature of individuals, those parents rarely manage to make kids stick forever to something they hate. A ban on cloning wouldn't abolish pushy parents.

One putatively scientific argument against cloning has been raised. As a National Public Radio commentator who opposes cloning quipped, "Diversity isn't just politically correct, it's good science." Sexual reproduction seems to have evolved for the purpose of staying ahead of ever-mutating pathogens in a continuing arms race. Novel combinations of genes created through sexual reproduction help immune systems devise defenses against rapidly evolving germs, viruses, and parasites. The argument against cloning says that if enough human beings were cloned, pathogens would likely adapt and begin to get the upper hand, causing widespread disease. The analogy often cited is what happens when a lot of farmers all adopt the same corn hybrid. If the hybrid is highly susceptible to a particular bug, then the crop fails.

Even if someday millions of clones of one person existed, who is to say that novel technologies wouldn't by then be able to control human pathogens?

That warning may have some validity for cloned livestock, which may well have to live in environments protected from infectious disease. But it is unlikely that there will be millions of clones of one person. Genomic diversity would still be the rule for humanity. There might be more identical twins, triplets, etc., but unless there are millions of clones of one person, raging epidemics sweeping through hordes of human beings with identical genomes seem very unlikely.

But even if someday millions of clones of one person existed, who is to say that novel technologies wouldn't by then be able to control human pathogens? After all, it wasn't genetic diversity that caused typhoid, typhus, polio, or measles to all but disappear in the United States. It was modern sanitation and modern medicine.

There's no reason to think that a law against cloning would make much difference anyway. "It's such a simple technology, it won't be banable," says Engelhardt. "That's why God made offshore islands, so that anybody who wants to do it can have it done." Cloning would simply go underground and be practiced without legal oversight. This means that people who turned to cloning would not have recourse to the law to enforce contracts, ensure proper standards, and hold practitioners liable for malpractice.

Who is likely to be making the decisions about whether human cloning should be banned? When President Clinton appointed the National Bioethics Advisory Commission, his stated hope was that such a commission could come up with some sort of societal consensus about what we should do with cloning.

The problem with achieving and imposing such a consensus is that Americans live in a large number of disparate moral communities. "If you call up the Pope in Rome, do you think he'll hesitate?" asks Engelhardt. "He'll say, 'No, that's not the way that Christians reproduce.' And if you live Christianity of a Roman Catholic sort, that'll be a good enough answer. And if you're fully secular, it won't be a relevant answer at all.

And if you're in-between, you'll feel kind of generally guilty."

Engelhardt questions the efficacy of such commissions: "Understand why all such commissions are frauds. Imagine a commission that really represented our political and moral diversity. It would have as its members Jesse Jackson, Jesse Helms, Mother Teresa, Bella Abzug, Phyllis Schlafly. And they would all talk together, and they would never agree on anything. . . . Presidents and Congresses rig—manufacture fraudulently—a consensus by choosing people to serve on such commissions who already more or less agree. . . . Commissions are created to manufacture the fraudulent view that we have a consensus."

Unlike Engelhardt, Fletcher believes that the National Bioethics Advisory Commission can be useful, but he acknowledges that "all of the commissions in the past have made recommendations that have had their effects in federal regulations. So they are a source eventually of regulations." The bioethics field is littered with ill-advised bans, starting in the mid-1970s with the two-year moratorium on recombining DNA and including the law against selling organs and blood and Clinton's recent prohibition on using human embryos in federally funded medical research.

Do not rush to ban cloning

As history shows, many bioethicists succumb to the thrill of exercising power by saying no. Simply leaving people free to make their own mistakes will get a bioethicist no perks, no conferences, and no power. Bioethicists aren't the ones suffering, the ones dying, and the ones who are infertile, so they do not bear the consequences of their bans. There certainly is a role for bioethicists as advisers, explaining to individuals what the ramifications of their decisions might be. But bioethicists should have no ability to stop individuals from making their own decisions, once they feel that they have enough information.

Ultimately, biotechnology is no different from any other technology—humans must be allowed to experiment with it in order to find its best uses and, yes, to make and learn from mistakes in using it. Trying to decide in advance how a technology should be used is futile. The smartest commission ever assembled simply doesn't have the creativity of millions of human beings trying to live the best lives that they can by trying out and developing new technologies.

So why is the impulse to ban cloning so strong? "We haven't gotten over the nostalgia for the Inquisition," concludes Engelhardt. "We are people who are post-modernist with a nostalgia for the Middle Ages. We still want the state to have the power of the Inquisition to enforce good public morals on everyone, whether they want it or not."

Organizations to Contact

The editors have compiled the following list of organizations concerned with the issues debated in this book. The descriptions are derived from materials provided by the organizations. All have publications or information available for interested readers. The list was compiled on the date of publication of the present volume; names, addresses, phone and fax numbers, and e-mail and Internet addresses may change. Be aware that many organizations take several weeks or longer to respond to inquiries, so allow as much time as possible.

American Association for Laboratory Animal Science (AALAS)
70 Timber Creek, Suite 5
Cordova, TN 38018-4233
(901) 754-8620
fax: (901) 753-0046
e-mail: info@aalas.org
Internet: http://www.aalas.org

The AALAS is concerned with the production, care, and study of laboratory animals. The organization provides a medium for the exchange of scientific information on all phases of laboratory animal care and use through its educational activities and certification programs. The association publishes two bimonthlies, the newsletter *AALAS Bulletin* and the journal *Laboratory Animal Science*.

American Civil Liberties Union (ACLU)
125 Broad St.
New York, NY 10004-2400
(212) 549-2500
publications: (800) 775-ACLU (2258)
e-mail: aclu@aclu.org
Internet: http://www.aclu.org

The ACLU champions the civil rights provided by the U.S. Constitution. Its members are becoming increasingly concerned that genetic testing may lead to genetic discrimination in the workplace—the refusal to hire or the termination of employees who are at risk for developing genetic conditions. The ACLU publishes a variety of handbooks, pamphlets, reports, and newsletters, including the quarterly *Civil Liberties* and the monthly *Civil Liberties Alert*.

American Life League (ALL)
PO Box 1350
Stafford, VA 22555
(703) 659-4171
fax: (703) 659-2586
e-mail: sysop@aol.org

ALL is an educational pro-life organization that opposes abortion, artificial contraception, reproductive technologies, and fetal experimentation. It asserts that it is immoral to perform experiments on living human embryos

78

and fetuses, whether inside or outside the mother's womb. ALL further contends that surrogate motherhood is contrary to moral law and violates the sanctity of marriage. Its publications include the policy statement *Creating a Pro-Life America*, the paper *What Is Norplant?* and the booklet *Contraceptive Compromise: The Perfect Crime*.

American Medical Association (AMA)
515 N. State St.
Chicago, IL, 60610
(312) 464-5000
Internet: http://www.ama-assn.org

The AMA is the largest and most prestigious professional association for medical doctors. It helps set standards for medical education and practices and is a powerful lobby in Washington for physicians' interests. The association publishes monthly journals for many medical fields, including the *Archives of Surgery*, as well as the weekly *JAMA*.

American Society of Human Genetics (ASHG)
9650 Rockville Pike
Bethesda, MD 20814-3998
(301) 571-1825
fax: (301) 530-7079
Internet: http://www.pslgroup.com

The ASHG is a professional society of physicians, researchers, genetic counselors, and others interested in human genetics. Committees within the organization deal with issues concerning the Human Genome Project, human genetics education, public policy, and social issues. The ASHG publishes the monthly *American Journal of Human Genetics*.

American Society of Law, Medicine, and Ethics (ASLME)
765 Commonwealth Ave.
Suite 1634, Boston, MA 02215
(617) 262-4990
fax: (617) 437-7596
Internet: http://www.aslme.org

The society's members include physicians, attorneys, health care administrators, and others interested in the relationship between law, medicine, and ethics. It takes no positions but acts as a forum for discussion of issues such as genetic engineering. The organization has an information clearinghouse and a library. It publishes the quarterlies *American Journal of Law* and *Journal of Law, Medicine, and Ethics;* the periodic *ASLME Briefings;* and books.

Association of Biotechnology Companies (ABC)
1666 Connecticut Ave. NW, Suite 330
Washington, DC 20009-1039
(202) 234-3330
fax: (202) 234-3565
Internet: http://www.oxbridge.com

The ABC provides information on biotechnology issues pertaining to regulations, patents, and finances. Its publications include the bimonthly newsletter *Association of Biotechnology Companies* and the periodic *ABC Letters*.

BC Biotechnology Alliance (BCBA)
1122 Mainland St., #450
Vancouver, BC V6B 5L1
CANADA
(604) 689-5602
fax: (604) 689-5603
Internet: http://www.biotech.pc.ca/bcba/

The BCBA is an association for producers and users of biotechnology. The alliance works to increase public awareness and understanding of biotechnology, including the awareness of its potential contributions to society. The alliance's publications include the bimonthly newsletter *Biofax* and the annual *Directory of BC Biotechnology Capabilities.*

Biotechnology Industry Organization (BIO)
1625 K St. NW, #1100
Washington, DC 20006
(202) 857-0244
fax: (202) 857-0237
Internet: http://www.bio.org

BIO is composed of companies engaged in industrial biotechnology. It monitors government actions that affect biotechnology and promotes increased public understanding of biotechnology through its educational activities and workshops. Its publications include the bimonthly newsletter *BIO Bulletin,* the periodic *BIO News,* and the book *Biotech for All.*

Center for Biomedical Ethics
PO Box 33 UMHC
Minneapolis, MN 55455
(612) 625-4917

The center seeks to advance and disseminate knowledge concerning ethical issues in health care and the life sciences. It conducts original research, offers educational programs, fosters public discussion and debate, and assists in the formulation of public policy. The center publishes a quarterly newsletter and reading packets on specific topics, including fetal tissue research.

Council for Responsible Genetics
5 Upland Rd., Suite 3
Cambridge, MA 02140
(617) 868-0870
fax: (617) 864-5164
Internet: http://www.fbresearch.org

The council is a national organization of scientists, health professionals, trade unionists, women's health activists, and others who work to ensure that biotechnology is developed safely and in the public interest. The council publishes the bimonthly newsletter *GeneWatch* and position papers on the Human Genome Project, genetic discrimination, germ-line modifications, and DNA-based identification systems.

Foundation for Biomedical Research
818 Connecticut Ave. NW
Washington, DC 20006
(202) 457-0654

The foundation supports humane animal research and serves to inform and educate the public about the necessity and importance of laboratory animals in biomedical research and testing. It publishes a bimonthly newsletter, videos, films, and numerous background papers, including *The Use of Animals in Biomedical Research and Testing* and *Caring for Laboratory Animals.*

Foundation on Economic Trends
1130 17th St. NW, #630
Washington, DC 20036
(202) 466-2823
fax: (202) 429-9602

The foundation examines the environmental, economic, and social consequences of genetic engineering. It believes society should use extreme caution when implementing genetic technologies to avoid endangering people, animals, and the environment. The foundation publishes the books *Biological Warfare: Deliberate Release of Microorganisms* and *Reproductive Technology* as well as articles and research reports.

Genetics Society of America
9650 Rockville Pike
Bethesda, MD 20814
(301) 571-1825
fax: (301) 530-7079

The society promotes professional cooperation among persons working in genetics and related sciences. It publishes the monthly journal *Genetics.*

Hastings Center
255 Elm Rd.
Briarcliff Manor, NY 10510
(914) 762-8500

Since its founding in 1969, the Hastings Center has played a pivotal role in exploring the medical, ethical, and social ramifications of biomedical advances. The center publishes books, papers, guidelines, and the bimonthly *Hastings Center Report.*

Health Resources and Services Administration
Dept. of Health and Human Services, Genetic Services
5600 Fishers Ln.
Rockville, MD 20857
(301) 443-1080
fax: (301) 443-4842
Internet: http://www.hrsa.dhhs.gov

The administration provides funds to develop or enhance regional and state genetic screening, diagnostic, counseling, and follow-up programs. It also provides funds to develop community-based psychological and social services for adolescents with genetic disorders. It has many publications available through its educational programs, and it produces directories and bibliographies on human genetics.

Incurably Ill for Animal Research
PO Box 1873
Bridgeview, IL 60455
(708) 598-7787

This organization consists of people who have incurable diseases and are concerned that the use of animals in medical research will be stopped or severely limited by animal rights activists, thus delaying or preventing the development of new cures. It publishes the monthly *Bulletin* and a quarterly newsletter.

International Genetics Federation (IGF)
University of British Columbia, Dept. of Botany
6270 University Blvd.
Vancouver, BC V6T 1Z4
CANADA
(604) 822-5629
fax: (604) 822-9179

Through its international network of genetics societies, the IGF works to further the science of genetics. The federation provides information about genetics and offers referrals to local genetics societies.

Kennedy Institute of Ethics
Georgetown University
1437 37th St. NW
Washington, DC 20057
(202) 687-8099
library: (800) 633-3849
fax: (202) 687-6779
Internet: http://guweb.georgetown.edu/kennedy/

The institute sponsors research on medical ethics, including ethical issues surrounding the use of recombinant DNA and human gene therapy. It supplies the National Library of Medicine with an on-line database on bioethics and publishes an annual bibliography in addition to reports and articles on specific issues concerning medical ethics.

March of Dimes Birth Defects Foundation
1901 L St. NW, #206
Washington, DC 20036
(202) 659-1800
fax: (202) 296-2964

The March of Dimes is concerned with preventing and treating birth defects, including those caused by genetic abnormalities. It monitors legislation and regulations that affect health care and research, awards grants for research, and provides funding for treatment of birth defects. The organization offers information on a wide variety of genetic diseases and their treatments, and it publishes the quarterly newsletter *Genetics in Practice*.

National Association for Biomedical Research (NABR)
818 Connecticut Ave. NW, Suite 303
Washington, DC 20006
(202) 857-0540
fax: (202) 659-1902
Internet: http://www.nabr.org

The NABR comprises universities, research institutes, professional societies, animal breeders and suppliers, and pharmaceutical companies that use animals for biomedical research and testing. The association also monitors and, if necessary, attempts to influence government legislation regarding the use of animals in research and testing. Its publications include the *NABR Update,* published biweekly, and the *NABR Alert,* published six to ten times a year.

National Institutes of Health (NIH)
Health and Human Services Dept., Human Genome Research
9000 Rockville Pike
Bethesda, MD 20892
(301) 402-0911
fax: (301) 402-0837
Internet: http://www.nih.gov

The NIH plans, coordinates, and reviews the progress of the Human Genome Project and works to improve techniques for cloning, storing, and handling DNA. It offers a variety of information on the Human Genome Project.

People for the Ethical Treatment of Animals (PETA)
501 Front St.
Norfolk, VA 23510
(757) 622-7382
Internet: http://www.peta-online.org

PETA is an educational and activist group that opposes all forms of animal exploitation. It conducts rallies and demonstrations to focus attention on animal experimentation, the fur fashion industry, and the killing of animals for human consumption—three issues it considers institutionalized cruelty. PETA hopes to educate the public about human chauvinist attitudes toward animals and about the conditions in slaughterhouses and research laboratories. It publishes reports on animal experimentation and animal farming and the quarterly newsletter *PETA's Animal Times.*

Society for the Study of Social Biology (SSSB)
c/o Jacci L. Rodgers
Oklahoma City University
Meinders School of Business
Oklahoma City, OK 73106
(405) 521-5824
fax: (405) 225-4511
Internet: http://www.okcu.edu/

The SSSB is an association of biological, behavioral, and social science scholars interested in the study of heredity and population. It promotes discussion, advancement, and sharing of knowledge about the biological and sociocultural forces affecting human population and their evolution. The society publishes the quarterly journal *Social Biology.*

Bibliography

Books

Kenneth W. Adolph, ed.   *Gene and Chromosome Analysis*. San Diego: Academic Press, 1994.

T.A. Brown   *Gene Cloning: An Introduction*. 3rd. ed. New York: Chapman and Hall, 1995.

Bill Clinton   "Cloning Prohibition Act of 1997: Message from the President of the United States Transmitting a Draft of Proposed Legislation to Prohibit Any Attempt to Create a Human Being Using Somatic Cell Nuclear Transfer to Provide for Further Review of the Ethical and Scientific Issues." Washington, DC: GPO, 1997.

D.J.A. Crommelin and H. Schellekens, eds.   *From Clone to Clinic*. Boston: Kluwer Academic, 1990.

Karl Drlica   *Understanding DNA and Gene Cloning: A Guide for the Curious*. 3rd. ed. New York: Wiley, 1997.

D.M. Glover and B.D. Hames, eds.   *DNA Cloning: A Practical Approach*. 2nd. ed. New York: IRL Press, 1995.

Nabil G. Hagig and Michael V. Viola, eds.   *Chromosome Microdissection and Cloning: A Practical Guide*. San Diego: Academic Press, 1993.

Christopher Howe   *Gene Cloning and Manipulation*. New York: Cambridge University Press, 1995.

Gérard Lucotte and François Baneyx   *Introduction to Molecular Cloning Techniques*. New York: VCH Publishers, 1993.

Bernard V. Perbal   *A Practical Guide to Molecular Cloning*. 2nd. ed. New York: Wiley, 1988.

Brian C. Schaefer, ed.   *Gene Cloning and Analysis: Current Innovations*. Portland, OR: Horizon Scientific Press, 1997.

Stuart C. Sealfon, ed.   *Receptor Molecular Biology*. San Diego: Academic Press, 1995.

U.S. Senate Committee on Labor and Human Resources   *Scientific Discoveries in Cloning: Challenges for Public Policy: Hearing Before the Subcommittee on Public Health and Safety of the Committee on Labor and Human Resources, United States Senate*, 105th Cong., 1st sess, March 12, 1997.

Peter K. Vogt and Inder M. Verma, eds.   *Oncogene Techniques*. San Diego: Academic Press, 1995.

J.G. Williams and R.K. Patient   *Genetic Engineering*. Washington, DC: IRL Press, 1988.

Dominic W.S. Wong — *The ABC's of Gene Cloning.* New York: Chapman and Hall, 1997.

Periodicals

Ken Adelman — "Ask Mr. Science," *Washingtonian,* September 1997.

Sharon Begley — "Little Lamb, Who Made Thee?" *Newsweek,* March 10, 1997.

Sharon Begley — "Spring Cloning," *Newsweek,* June 30, 1997.

John Carey — "The Biotechcentury," *Business Week,* March 10, 1997.

Kate Clinton — "Hello, Dolly!" *Progressive,* April 1997.

Commonweal — "Cloning Isn't Sexy," March 28, 1997.

Jean Bethke Elshtain — "Ewegenics," *New Republic,* March 31, 1997.

Kevin T. Fitzgerald — "Little Lamb, Who Made Thee?" *America,* March 29, 1997.

John Garvey — "The Mystery Remains," *Commonweal,* March 28, 1997.

Christine Gorman — "Neti and Ditto," *Time,* March 17, 1997.

Christine Gorman — "To Ban or Not to Ban?" *Time,* June 16, 1997.

Wray Herbert et al. — "The World After Cloning," *U.S. News & World Report,* March 10, 1997.

Ruth Hubbard — "Irreplaceable Ewe," *Nation,* March 24, 1997.

Jeffrey Kluger — "Will We Follow the Sheep?" *Time,* March 10, 1997.

Diana Lutz — "Hello, Hello, Dolly, Dolly," *Sciences,* May/June 1997.

National Review — "Cloning Cloning Cloning," March 24, 1997.

Elizabeth Pennisi and Nigel Williams — "Will Dolly Send In the Clones?" *Science,* March 7, 1997.

Stephen G. Post — "The Judeo-Christian Case Against Human Cloning," *America,* June 21–28, 1997.

Tabitha M. Powledge — "Good-bye, Dolly," *Technology Review,* May/June 1997.

Larry Reibstein and Gregory Beals — "A Cloned Chop, Anyone?" *Newsweek,* March 10, 1997.

William Safire — "Clone Clone Clone Clone," *New York Times Magazine,* April 6, 1997.

H.T. Shapiro — "Ethical and Policy Issues of Human Cloning," *Science,* July 11, 1997.

David Stipp — "The Real Biotech Revolution," *Fortune,* March 31, 1997.

Alan Taylor — "Silence of the Lamb," *New Yorker,* March 17, 1997.

John Travis — "Ewe Again? Cloning from Adult DNA," *Science News,* March 1, 1997.

John Travis — "A Fantastical Experiment," *Science News,* April 5, 1997.

Lindsy Van Gelder — "Hello, Dolly, Hello, Dolly," *Ms.,* May/June 1997.

Allen Verhey	"Theology After Dolly," *Christian Century,* March 19–26, 1997.
Bruce Wallace	"The Dolly Debate," *Maclean's,* March 10, 1997.
Kenneth L. Woodward	"Today the Sheep," *Newsweek,* March 10, 1997.
World Press Review	"Of Sheep and Men," June 1997.

Index